ORIGINS
OF THE
NATURAL LAW
TRADITION

ORIGINS
OF THE
NATURAL LAW
TRADITION

ROBERT N. WILKIN

JOHN S. MARSHALL

THOMAS E. DAVITT, S.J.

ARTHUR L. HARDING

EDITED WITH AN INTRODUCTION BY
ARTHUR L. HARDING

KENNIKAT PRESS
Port Washington, N. Y./London

ORIGINS OF THE NATURAL LAW TRADITION

Copyright 1954 by Southern Methodist University Press
Reissued in 1971 by Kennikat Press by arrangement
Library of Congress Catalog Card No: 70-132083
ISBN 0-8046-1411-3

Manufactured by Taylor Publishing Company   Dallas, Texas

ESSAY AND GENERAL LITERATURE INDEX REPRINT SERIES

INTRODUCTION

CONCEPTS of a Law of Nature are as old as Western philosophy. From its inception Greek philosophy was concerned to reduce the apparent chaos and conflict of the visible world to some principle of harmony and order. The true relationship of man to the world about him was of primary concern. Philosophical solutions of these problems were found in concepts of Natural Law by which men could be brought into an ideal relationship with each other and with their environment.

Concepts of Natural Law are almost as varied as are the philosophical systems which have been evolved in the history of Western civilization. Each in turn has wrestled with the seemingly insoluble problem of the ideal society and its position in the cosmos. Some solutions have been essentially religious in nature; others have rested upon magnificent cosmologies. Some have sought the answer in comparative anthropology, the development of legal institutions in rudimentary and primitive societies; others in a *jus gentium*, the common legal experiences of contemporary societies. Still others have probed the mysteries of the physical universe via the natural sciences. In any event, the search continues.

The annual conferences on Law in Society, conducted by the Southern Methodist University School of Law and the Southwestern Legal Foundation, are devoted to the study of the relationship of legal doctrines and institutions to social institutions; the effect of social beliefs and needs and institutions upon the formulation of law, and the effect of legal doctrines and their administration upon the society. The accomplishment of such a task requires a re-examination of the Natural Law doctrine. For this there are several reasons.

In the first place, the persistence of the notion of Natural Law supports a possible inference of its validity, however questionable may be some of the methods employed and some of the contents developed. So far as the concept has validity, it must be considered in any contemporary legal doctrine. Secondly, a good deal of our existing legal doctrine can be explained historically only in the light of Natural Law doctrines which have prevailed in times past. In the third place, the average American believes strongly that there is such a thing as Natural Law and that he has natural rights. So long as laws are made by men and administered by men, this belief, ill-founded or no, is a sociological fact which the jurist must take into account. Finally, no legal theory, and no study of legal institutions today, can be confined to the territory of a particular sovereign; the law of other countries and the Law of Nations must be taken into account. Natural Law doctrines may offer means of *rapprochement* to the positive law of other countries. The Law of Nations, wanting a sovereign and a command theory of law, traditionally has abounded in Natural Law learning.

In studying Natural Law one must begin with definitions. The outstanding characteristic of most contemporary discussions of the subject is that there are about as many definitions and concepts represented as there are participants. Often the discussion is concluded without agreement even on fundamental terms.

Accordingly this, the 1953 Conference on Law in Society, was devoted to definition, to outlining four different ideas of Natural Law which have bulked large in our legal history. The four concepts presented do not cover even the major ones, but they are a beginning. Subsequent conferences will pursue the inquiry further.

In selecting the four theories of Natural Law it was thought advisable to explore only concepts of Natural Law as a manifestation of universal order, leaving for the future the subsidiary notions of Natural Rights developed in more recent centuries. The four theories have been presented in terms of their principal expositors: Cicero, with his transcending synthesis of the Aristotelian man and the Stoic cosmology; St. Thomas Aquinas, with his Hellenized adaptation of traditional Jewish-Christian theology; Richard Hooker, who provided an intellectual bridge between the neoclassical Natural Law of Bracton, of John of Salisbury, and of Anglican theology, and the rationalist Natural Rights doctrines of the seventeenth century; and Herbert Spencer, who constructed a sort of Natural Law on the basis of the natural laws of biological existence as propounded by Charles Darwin.

The University is in great debt to the speakers who participated in the 1953 Conference. Judge Wilkin is a lifelong student of Roman history and legal philosophy, and is the author of *Eternal Lawyer: A Legal Biography of Cicero*. Father Davitt is trained in psychology and law and is the author of *The Nature of Law*, an analysis of the conflict of Will versus Reason in medieval legal thinking. Professor Marshall is an authority upon Anglican church history and doctrine and English philosophy of the Tudor period.

He has performed a valuable service in publishing an edition of the major parts of Hooker's *Ecclesiastical Polity* rendered in modern English.

Mr. Dwight L. Simmons of the Dallas Bar, long a student of legal philosophy, contributed greatly to the success of the Conference, not only by financial support but also by participation in the program.

ARTHUR L. HARDING

The School of Law
Southern Methodist University

CONTENTS

CICERO AND THE
LAW OF NATURE

Robert N. Wilkin

THE conditions today which cause a revival of interest in Natural Law are the same conditions that inspired the Greeks to perceive and formulate the principles of Natural Law as part of their philosophy during the fourth century B.C.[1] Similar conditions prompted the Romans to make Natural Law the basis of their jurisprudence during the last century of the Republic. The same general conditions made it necessary for the Scholastic philosophers to base their theory of the state on Natural Law when Europe was emerging from the anarchy of the Dark Ages. Similar conditions impelled the Founding Fathers of our country to make Natural Law the cornerstone of the constitutional government which they established.[2]

The conditions that existed at each of these periods of history were the conditions that always confront mankind at a time of great political transition. Whenever military or commercial expansion or political evolution makes the old, customary, local government insufficient for the needs of the time and creates a necessity for a new form of government which can rule over different localities, different nations, and different races, then men are compelled to search for the true principles of law and order. Because they prefer rational government to arbitrary power and lawful order to strife and violence, men are impelled to consider human nature and try to discover those principles of individual and social life which are not arbitrary, local, or temporal, but rational, universal, and eternal—and that effort leads to Natural Law.

Cicero and the Republic

Coming now to the specific subject of this discussion—Origins of the Natural Law Tradition—it is well that the men who made the program for this Conference had it begin with a study of the time and influence of Cicero. It was during his lifetime, and the last years of the Republic, that the science of jurisprudence was developed; and Cicero, as lawyer, magistrate, statesman, and author, then gave Natural Law a definition and statement of principles which have been quoted with approval by scholars, philosophers, and jurists down to our time.

FOUR CONSIDERATIONS

In order to understand Cicero's contribution to Natural Law it is necessary to have a fairly clear perception of four preliminary considerations: (1) the political conditions during the last years of the Roman Republic; (2) the general character of Roman Law and its system of administration at that time; (3) the fundamental principles of Stoic philosophy; and (4) some of the important things that Cicero said and wrote about Natural Law.

We shall give attention to those considerations in that order.

I. Political Conditions

The active years of Cicero's life were the last years

of the Roman Republic. During that time private law attained a high development and the foundations of Roman jurisprudence were established, but at the same time public law disintegrated and civil government failed. We must consider Cicero's life and work against that strange and paradoxical background.

Rome had at first a city government, which in time became a national government, and now Rome was the capital that ruled the world. But in form and substance it had not changed much. It was trying to meet the responsibilities of world government with the equipment of a city-state. Rome had been a kingdom, an aristocracy, an oligarchy, a republic, and now, through the action of its great military commanders and dictators, it was becoming an empire.

As long as the Romans had a foreign enemy that threatened them, they stood together at home. Their domestic evolution had been accomplished by peaceful means. The plebeians, who at first had no participation in government, finally became eligible for all offices and controlled the legislative assembly. And this great change was accomplished without civil war or violence, so great was the respect of Romans for law and lawful procedure. But after the Second Punic War class strife began at home. The patience, perseverance, and unity which overcame Hannibal completely disappeared when Romans began to contend with Romans.[3]

The disintegration of the Republican constitution may be said to have begun with Tiberius and Gaius Gracchus. The reforms which the Gracchi had proposed were worthy and needed, but the Gracchi made the mistake of furthering them by unconstitutional methods. This forced their opponents, the members of the oligarchy and the senatorial or aristocratic party, to resort to force and violence. As a result of such unlawful strife, both the Gracchi were killed and Rome experienced the first political proscription. Three thousand followers were executed. The victors said the Gracchi were to be made an example. The result was, however, that they were made martyrs; men worshiped their images. Their cause, though temporarily retarded, was soon revived, and measures which had been proposed by them were carried into effect.

That was the beginning of the factional strife between the aristocratic and popular classes, between the senatorial and capitalist parties, between the Roman citizens and the people of the Italian provinces, and all the various alignments of these and other groups which characterized, if they did not cause, the disintegration of the Roman Republic. It caused the horrible and devastating Social War, the Civil War, the dictatorship of Marius and his cruel proscription, the dictatorship of Sulla and the Great Proscription, and led directly to the Triumvirate and the dictatorship of Caesar, which set the stage for the advent of Octavius, Caesar Augustus, the first Emperor.

Effect on Cicero. Cicero was in his teens during the dictatorship of Marius. He was a young man beginning the practice of his profession during the dictatorship of Sulla. His famous defense of Roscius occurred during Sulla's dictatorship. It was his first great lament for the disintegration of the Republic and its civil order. His oration was his first professional challenge of arbitrary government—his first ardent appeal for the restoration of lawful authority. He spoke with such vehemence against the Proscription that he finally had to flee to Athens for safety. After Sulla's death he returned to Rome. The rest of his public life was a futile effort to restore the Republic, to revive the dignity and power of the Senate, to substitute law for force, or as he said, "make audacity yield to authority."

Sulla had tried to restore the aristocracy to authority. But he found there was no longer any aristocracy. The standards, the discipline, the devotion of the ancient aristocrats had been lost in the general corruption of government, morals, and manners at Rome. Furthermore, he could not escape the fact that restoration of order by despotic decree or the establishment of law by violence is impossible.[4]

About the last wholesome activity of the Republic was during Cicero's term as Consul. Under his leadership, encouragement, and protection the Senate exerted its power for constitutional government. At that time Cicero suppressed the Catalinarian rebellion which threatened Rome with another reign of terror. Cicero, as he said, made arms yield to authority. He then tried diligently to make the rule of law permanent by re-establishing constitutional government on a consensus of good citizens, *Concordia Ordinum* as he called it.

When his term of office expired, however, he discovered that there was no consensus and that there were too few good citizens, for the same reason that Sulla had discovered for the lack of an aristocracy. Devotion and discipline were gone. Without authority of office Cicero was powerless against the machinations and lawlessness of his enemies. Clodius incited the thugs and gangsters of Rome to insult and threaten Cicero on the streets, and finally he persuaded the popular assembly to pass a resolution of banishment against Cicero. Again the great lawyer had to seek refuge in Athens.

In order to maintain some civil authority in Rome it was necessary for Pompey, Crassus, and Caesar to organize the First Triumvirate. Within the next year, however, the Triumvirs began to feel the need of Cicero's influence for law and order. With their approval the Senate passed a resolution for his recall which was promptly approved by the Comitia. Cicero's return was not unconditional. He was obliged to support the Triumvirate. He has been accused of inconsistency for doing so. But, like Cato, he had learned by hard experience that "any government is better than no government."

While Cicero supported measures sponsored by the Triumvirate, he did not forsake the Republic. He still hoped that the Republican constitution might be restored. To that end he wrote his *De Re Publica*. He also wrote *De Legibus,* although the latter work was not published until after his death. These two works are cited today as authority for constitutional and lawful government as against arbitrary government of individual, class, or populace. His forthright, logical, and convincing arguments were futile, however, against the trend of his times.

Caesar and Cicero. After the death of Crassus the rivalry between Pompey and Caesar soon developed into open warfare. Those two great Romans knew that conditions in Rome required a military dictator, and each determined that he should exercise that power. The absolute need of military dictatorship was made clear by the conditions which Caesar found when he and his veterans entered the city. When Rome was abandoned by Pompey, the consuls, and the senators, the mobs broke loose. Civilians hid themselves, knowing that they would be killed if they should be seen. Women had their clothing torn from them in the streets, and children wandered aimlessly about the city. The most terrible crimes went unpunished. All whose sensibilities were wounded by such spectacles were anxious for a strong and durable government. As G. P. Baker has said, "How far civilization really does depend on mere law and order we only realize in times of anarchy."[5] Romans were not then concerned about the kind of government. Any authority that could give security to life and property would be welcome. The devolution which delivered Rome to a dictator had been accomplished before Caesar assumed control.

Caesar's opponents who continued to bear arms were pursued relentlessly to their utter destruction. But Caesar published no proscribed lists in Rome. He had witnessed the futility of the reprisals of Marius and Sulla. He said, "Let us introduce another way of conquering and seek our safety in clemency." Those who sought his favor received it promptly and were welcomed back into the political life of Rome. There is abundant proof of Caesar's desire to establish a government of law. Events had proved the statesman-like and prophetic character of a statement which he had made to the Senate some years before: "Whenever in the past the great bulwark of the law has been weakened, the consequences have invariably been calamitous. If by any act it should now be seriously impaired, the danger is that it may be ultimately completely overthrown, to the disaster of all within the state." Caesar's attitude toward the law, his leniency to former opponents, and particularly his generous and gracious attitude toward Cicero, made it easy for Cicero to acquiesce in Caesar's administration. Cicero's conduct at that time exemplifies the precept of Protagoras that one should always support those who champion the law.

It is interesting to contemplate what might have been accomplished for world order if Caesar's life had been spared and if he and Cicero could have worked together for a constitutional government for the entire Roman dominion of that day. Both men had a profound understanding of the purpose of law in society. Caesar was a man of action, Cicero a philosopher. They were both statesmen, literary artists, and men of great mental power. Together they might have established a system of world law and a method of administration. Had they done so, what untold suffering by future generations would have been averted!

Caesar's magnetic personality and military genius were the forces that held the Roman government together. His assassination immediately dissipated all civil discipline. Confusion and conflict broke out, not only in Rome, but throughout the Roman world. The military forces that had conquered the world were again thrown into internecine war to conquer Rome for themselves. One of these forces was directed by Antony. This crisis set the stage for the final act of Cicero's life. In view of the conditions obtaining at the time, he could, in good conscience, support the rule of men like Pompey and Caesar. They were men of principle and entertained a hearty respect for the principles which Cicero espoused. 'But Cicero

could never acquiesce in the domination of a dema-
gogue and libertine like Antony. With full knowledge of the risk which he assumed, he threw the full
weight of his personality and powers against Antony.
He delivered his last orations, known as the Philip-
pics, and exhorted the Senate to assume command of
the Roman government and defend its constitution.
He said, "I who have always been a counsellor of
peace am against peace with Antony."

To the senators he said, "We have stood against
the weapons of traitors, but we still must wrest those
weapons from their hands. If we cannot do this, I will
speak as becomes a senator and a Roman—let us die."
Cicero was the very soul of opposition to autocracy.
He represented the law, Antony represented force.
He represented the moral order of life, Antony arbitrary will. Cicero knew that if Antony were not
destroyed all hope for the Republic would be gone
and with it would go the liberties of Romans. Future
generations who suffered the tyranny of such emperors
as Nero learned too late what Cicero had tried to
prevent.

When Octavius and Lepidus went over to Antony
with their legions and formed the perfidious Second
Triumvirate, Cicero's fate, together with the fate of
the Republic, was sealed. His name appeared on the
proscribed list, and his head was soon affixed to the
Rostra. Law was abandoned in the Eternal City and
the Eternal Lawyer was sacrificed. That which had
been the living head of the Republic was now the
death mask of the Republic. But what Cicero had said
and written became the inspiration of all future republics.

II. Roman Law

In contrast to the collapse of public law, let us consider the accomplishments in private law. The early law of Rome was "customary law," a law of tradition handed down from generation to generation by those early Romans whose essential quality had been an austere and unflinching devotion to the community and to the law and its discipline.[6]

In early times this law was interpreted and administered by priests, the pontifices. As Rome grew and its influence expanded there was an insistent demand for a codification of law, a statement of principles which would make the law available to all. A commission was appointed to prepare such a statement, and in a short time the Twelve Tables were posted in the Forum. At that early time Rome had legal statesmen who could put the principles of law in clear and concise terms.[7]

But codes stand still and life moves on. Although the Twelve Tables stood for centuries as the basic statutory law, a kind of Magna Carta, there was an ever growing need to reform and modify the primitive law to meet Rome's expanding life. Some change was made by legislation, but by far the greater part of adjustment and growth was accomplished by interpretation and the praetors' edicts. In both methods the influence of lawyers, the jurisconsults, controlled.

History does not afford us all the details of the change from pontifical to professional jurisprudence. We know, however, that with the publication of the Twelve Tables the law became public, and thereafter the opinions and forms prescribed by the priests were no longer secret. In time Claudius and his secretary

Flavius collected the forms, decisions, and opinions and published a work on actions, precedents, and the calendar. With that work as authority, men of experience and study in the law were soon issuing their own opinions (*Responsa*), and soon thereafter they were expounding the questions and answers arising in their practice before the younger men who were desirous of learning the law. That was the beginning of the legal profession.

The character of the work done by these lawyers induced Romans generally to give great respect to the functions of the consulting lawyer. The opinions of such jurisconsults became one of the sources of legal authority. The expansion of legal administration from city to national and then to international needs quite naturally placed more and more authority in public officers. The bulk of judicial work was finally entrusted to the praetors, and when Rome became the capital of the world and all trade routes led to Rome, special courts had to be provided for the determination of rights and liabilities arising under the varied laws of other nations. There was then established the office of *praetor inter cives et peregrinos* for the determination of controversies between citizens and foreigners.[8]

The judicial power was never entirely separated from other functions of government in Rome. The magistrates exercised both judicial authority (*jurisdictio*) and administrative power (*imperium*); but as stated, most of the judicial work was entrusted to the praetors. In the ordinary course of procedure the praetor would perform first the functions which are performed today by the judge at the pretrial conference. He would determine whether there was a justiciable question, and if so, would state the law to be applied to the case. He would state the issue and then refer the case to an arbitrator for its determination. Finally he would enter judgment on the decision of the arbitrator.

The praetors came in time to exercise what we would call equitable jurisdiction. They determined in what cases strict law should give way to natural justice (*naturalis aequitas*). They performed much the same function that chancery courts performed later in England. By far the greatest influence of the praetors, however, was exercised through the edict. The edict was the praetor's annual announcement of his intentions in respect to his judicial administration. This power to modify judicial procedure, and as a consequence the law itself, was at first a custom, but in time it obtained legislative sanction.[9]

The political, economic, social, and intellectual changes of the last century of the Republic could not be provided for by mere interpretation of the old law. New law and new forms of action were required. A remarkable evolution in private law was at that time accomplished, and in great part it was done through the praetor's edict. Many of the praetors were not lawyers. For assistance in drafting of their edicts, therefore, they turned to the respected jurisconsults. Each successive edict would copy much of the previous edicts, but from time to time additions and changes were made.

During this period the fundamental principles of Roman jurisprudence were established. Although it was a rapid and at times a radical development, there was no break in juristic tradition. Early in the process the legal praetors and jurisconsults developed the art of extracting the true principles from the strict and literal statements of the statutes and prior decisions. This juristic method, the main categories of juristic thought, and the fundamental legal institutions were established in the last years of the Republic, although the refinement of Roman law was not perfected until the second and third centuries of the Empire. It is a remarkable social phenomenon that private law continued to grow and improve in spite of the disintegration and confusion of public law and administration during the same period.[10]

Ius Gentium. When the Roman armies had extended their dominion over the whole Mediterranean area, it became necessary for the *pro-praetor* in each subject country and the *praetor peregrinus* in Rome to interpret and administer the laws of other lands. They discovered then that there were certain universal and eternal principles of equity and justice common to all legal systems. They referred to these principles as *ius gentium*: the law of peoples or world law. This law was based upon that reason and that innate sense of right and justice common in all races. Two characteristics of this law were (a) the rule of good faith and (b) the determination of the effects of acts by the intention of the parties and not merely by the words used. All of the principles and institutions of *ius gentium* were the product of native Roman jurisprudence stimulated by the circumstances of the newly acquired empire.

The same period which saw the development of *ius gentium* saw also the beginning of the reign of Greek thought in Rome. The great Roman lawyers of that period were students of Greek philosophy. The Greek doctrine of Natural Law found its entry into Roman legal thought at the same time that Roman experience had developed the principles common to all peoples. The philosophic basis which Greek thought furnished for the universality of the principles of *ius gentium* served in all departments of the law as a strong support of rationalism against traditionalism and of ethical as opposed to strictly legal principles.

The principles of Stoicism supplied the practical need of Romans by supporting the rules which their experience had evolved as part of the *ius gentium.* Cicero was an ardent champion of Stoic principles and found in their application to law a firm rationalization of his political aims and ideals. Cicero translated much of the Greek philosophy into Latin and invented Latin terms for concepts which had not previously appeared in Latin literature. In order to understand Natural Law of that period and its impress on Roman jurisprudence it is necessary to have some understanding of the fundamental principles of Stoic philosophy.

III. Stoic Philosophy

The Stoic school was founded by Zeno, a Phoenician who is presumed to have been subjected to some Semitic influence and may have obtained some ideas from oriental savants or Hebrew prophets. Stoicism at first inculcated a stern abnegation and detachment from the world in order that perception and judgment might be free from passion. Its ideal was the sage who ordered his life by reason and insight into man's essential nature. While the Stoics always remained individualists, by Cicero's time and under Roman influence they had begun to extol proper social impulses and obligations.[11]

The core of Stoicism was Ethics. With ideas borrowed from Socrates, Plato, and Aristotle, Stoicism became the very antithesis of the cynicism and subjectivism of the Sophists and Skeptics, the positivists of that day.[12] The Stoics taught that there were empirical standards of truth and justice which were revealed to man through right reason according to nature. Right reason and the law of nature which holds sway throughout the universe were one. Law also had its basis in nature. Man has an inborn notion of right and wrong, the Stoics taught, and law in its very essence rests not upon the arbitrary will of a ruler or upon the emotional decree of a multitude, but upon nature and the innate ideas of man's moral nature. To live with religious devotion in harmony with oneself according to one's rational nature in obedience to universal law—such was the ethical teaching of Stoicism.

The Stoic belief in a cosmic mind or world soul which governs the universe, not arbitrarily, but in accordance with law which has been made available to man through reason, is harmonious with the concept of the great modern physical scientists that (as Sir James Jeans says) "the stream of knowledge is heading toward a nonmechanical reality; the universe begins to look more like a great thought than like a great machine."[13] If we apply to the Stoics the admonition "By their fruits ye shall know them," then they must be given credit not only for Cicero and the jurisconsults of the Republican era, but for many of the great jurists of the imperial age, as well as for such outstanding figures as Seneca, Epictetus, and the Emperor Marcus Aurelius, whose *Meditations* has been acclaimed "the high-water mark of unassisted virtue."

As George Sabine has said, the belief in Providence was for the Stoics essentially a belief in the value of social purposes and in the duty of man to bear a share of them:

The fundamental teaching of the Stoics was a religious conviction of the oneness and perfection of nature or a true moral order. A life according to nature meant for them resignation to the will of God, co-operation with all the forces of good, a sense of dependence upon a power above man that makes for righteousness, and the composure of mind that comes from faith in the goodness and reasonableness of the world.[14]

It is clear that in early as well as later times Stoic philosophy was "the intellectual support of men of political, moral, and religious convictions."[15] But what is most important for our present purpose, it was the inspiration and support of the jurists who founded Roman jurisprudence, which became the basis of law for the modern world. Stoicism could serve today as a common meeting-ground and rallying standard for all men and all races who oppose the atheistic, immoral, and destructive propaganda of the communistic revolutionaries.

IV. Cicero and Natural Law

Holding in mind what the political world was in Cicero's day, what the law and its administration was, and what the prevalent Stoic philosophy was, let us consider what Cicero said. His statements must be considered in the light of his times and his experiences. At the very time that Roman jurisprudence made its finest contribution to the science and philosophy of private law, that is, the law that governs men as individuals, Cicero saw public law and governmental administration fail and disintegrate. Cicero had given his life to the service of the Republic, and the greatest sorrow of his life was caused by its failure. He said he had grieved more over the loss of the Republic than a mother would grieve for the loss of her only son. But Rome, that had conquered the world, could not rule itself.

It is doubtful if any man was ever more aware of the tragedy of his time than was Cicero. He knew the glorious possibilities and he saw them destroyed in a maelstrom of conspiracy, tyranny, avarice, lust, and cruelty. Such a tragedy impelled his sensitive and informed mind to search through all history and philosophy for the true basis of peace and order in the world. He was a lawyer, and his study and practice had given him intimate knowledge as to what the law could do for men in their private affairs. He was more than a practicing lawyer, however, and more than a juristic writer — he was a legal statesman. He contemplated the law in its broadest aspects. He believed that true law could do for aggregations of men, cities, states, and nations what it had done for individuals.

He considered man's essential nature and his need for government and law. He inquired into the fundamentals of just government and the true source of law, its purpose, and its function. He put his theories and principles into practice as praetor and consul at Rome and as governor of Cilicia, and proved that his theories of government and of law were sound. The accomplishments of men like Scaevola,[16] Cato, Sulpicius, and Cicero as colonial governors had verified his statement, made in his oration for the Manilian Law, that there had been foreign countries which "preferred being subject to the Roman people rather than being themselves lords of their own nations." They preferred the Roman rule of law to the despotic rule of native kings. Where true law was established and honestly and fairly administered the people prospered and were satisfied.

Cicero's pronouncements on law are found in his orations, in his letters, and in such works as his essay on the commonwealth (*De Re Publica*), his essay on the laws (*De Legibus*), his essay on the ethics of citizenship (*De Officiis*), and excerpts quoted by later writers from works which have not been preserved.[17] His general philosophy of life and government is revealed in his Tusculan Disputations and his essay on divinity (*De Natura Deorum*).[18]

Government. Cicero as a true Stoic based his philosophy on the nature of man and the nature of the cosmos, and it led him to a belief in a Divine Creator. To him all creation was the handiwork of a divine intelligence, and it was designed according to plan and for some good purpose. Because man was the highest order of creation, Cicero concluded that his welfare was the purpose of creation. The excellency of man over all other types of being was apparent from the fact that man had been given a mind. He said the *Mundus* was not formed for trees or for animals but for the sake undoubtedly of those animated beings that exercised reason. He ridiculed the assertion that the sky and the earth were formed through the accidental concourse of a number of particles without the intermediation of any organizing principle. With something of the inspiration of the Psalmist he said that only those who had never gazed upon the sky could talk such nonsense. His views seem to be supported today by such

great physical scientists as Millikan, Jeans, and Edding-
ton. The important point, however, is that Cicero accepted the Stoic theory of a world soul, or God, who
was the ultimate sanction for law and morality. In his
defense of Cluentius, Cicero said, "The favor of Heaven
may be gained by duty done to God and man, and by
righteous prayers."

Upon the basis of his observations as to man's nature
and his belief in a moral order, Cicero constructed his
theory of government and man's obligation to the state.
Man was by nature sociable. This sociability, said
Cicero, is the outcome of what we are, a concomitant of
our being. And, said he, it is reason and language that
make this sociability possible. Because of the existence
of this common tie between all the members of the
human race, and because man was the object of
creation, the obligation rested upon every human being
not only to have a care for his fellows but to spare
himself no toil or trouble in his efforts to help others.
Failure to promote the universal sociability and well-
being he thought a violation of our nature (*repugnante
et adversante natura*). It is remarkable how closely his
theories approximate the doctrine of charity (*caritas*)
of the Christian teachers whom succeeding generations
were soon to hear in Rome. No wonder that Erasmus
felt that "a divinity inspired the man."

The paradox of life is, and always has been, that
men must give freely what they dare not and cannot
be coerced into giving. They must freely give their
lives in service of their fellow-men, but they must
resist with their very lives the attempt of any tyrant
or despot to subvert and subject their free will to any
form of statism or totalitarianism. Men cannot escape
their individual responsibility by any form of commu-

nism or state paternalism. Cicero opposed such political nostrums. Man is an individual but is also by nature sociable. The responsibilities resulting from these opposed phases of life cannot be avoided, because they are implicit in human nature.

In his works on the *Commonwealth* and the *Laws* Cicero carried his philosophy and his legal experience into politics. His *De Re Publica* and *De Legibus* are the first Roman contributions to the philosophy of politics. He recognized three basic forms of government — monarchy, aristocracy, and democracy. He recognized that each form had in it the seeds of decay. Life was always in a state of flux, and different forms of government came in succession. He had hoped that some permanence and security of government might be obtained by establishing a balance among the various elements of society. He thought stability might be attained by combining the best elements of the different forms of government. This arrangement was to be reached through agreement. It would be based upon the general will — not the will of any individual or faction, nor the popular will, but that public will which would result from civic devotion and the giving of free expression to the natural elements of society. Cicero was not a victim of the democratic fallacy that popular government would necessarily be just government, but he did believe that just government would be popular government.

Cicero recognized that just as a man has a higher self that controls his ordinary self, so the state should have a higher or permanent self, embodied in a constitution that would set bounds to its ordinary self as expressed by factions or public emotions at any particular moment. He said, "This constitution has a great measure of equibility without which men can hardly remain free for any length of time." This theory of balance and sovereignty of law inspired the founders of our nation. John Adams in his *Defence of the Constitutions of Government* said, "As all the ages of the world have not produced a greater statesman and philosopher united than Cicero, his authority should have great weight."

Law. Such being Cicero's conception of government, it was necessary then for him to give a definition of law and indicate its source and purpose. The object of government being the commonweal and justice, Cicero insisted that law was the essential means to that end. Law to him was the catalytic element in the social compound, the factional solvent, and the bond of unity of society. In his oration in defense of Cluentius he said:

Law is the bond which secures our privileges in the commonwealth, the foundation of our liberty, the fountainhead of justice. Within the law are reposed the mind and heart, the judgment and the conviction of the state. The state without law would be like the human body without a mind —unable to employ the parts which are to it as sinews, blood, and limbs. The magistrates who administer the law, the judges who interpret it — all of us in short — obey the law to the end that we may be free.

In *De Legibus* he said that the law is a silent magistrate and a magistrate the voice of the law. The law, therefore, was the most important aspect of government. Cicero considered it a reflection or imitation of divine and eternal law, the moral order revealed to man through his reason and conscience.

Cicero had practiced law too long, had acquired too much experience in politics and in the courts to have any confusion between the civil (or promulgated) law and the philosophy of law, between the positive law and the Law of Nature. He knew that in every state clashes of legal rights and interests were inevitable and that some practical legal system was therefore necessary if such disagreements were to be adjusted in an orderly and peaceable way. The maintenance of peace by process of law, he said repeatedly, was the only decent procedure for civilized beings. Such a system of law required a statement of rules in greater detail and with more precision than could be found in the concepts of Natural Law, but to him natural and positive law were not in conflict, but supported each other. He knew the sources of the positive law of the state. It took form in custom, legislation, decree, agreement, and judicial opinion. But he also recognized that underlying the positive law was a fundamental law or law of laws which had its origin in man's nature and should always be the rational, social, and moral norm or standard of positive law.

Moreover, Cicero recognized that written law is necessarily word-bound and limited, and that because it is a form of human expression, it exhibits imperfections. Law cannot be stated in advance so that it will cover all the diversities of life and human relationships. The positive law, therefore, must continually be adjusted to fit new conditions. The imperfections and gaps in the formal law had thus to be overcome by resort to the spirit of Natural Law. Cicero's ideas as to the origin of this Natural Law were expressed in his oration for the defense of Milo when he rationalized the right of self-defense. He said:

This therefore is a law, Oh judges, not written, but born with us, which we have not learned, or received by tradition, or read, but which we have taken, absorbed and imbibed from nature herself; a law which we were not taught, but to which we were made, which we were not trained in, but which is ingrained in us, namely, that if our life be in danger from plots or from open violence, or from the weapons of robbers or enemies, every means of securing our safety is honorable.

The term Natural Law has, from the beginning, represented three different concepts: (1) It is used sometimes to express the idea of legal philosophy — that philosophy of law which champions the principles of natural and moral law. (2) It is used also to cover generally accepted principles of equity, *ius gentium,* common law, and the like. (3) It is also used to express a certain standard, critique, or norm for the analysis and judgment of positive law.

Cicero in his *De Re Publica* gave a definition of Natural Law which has been accepted by scholars down to the present day. Professor McIlwain has said that Cicero's definition is one of the most memorable statements in all political literature. Said Cicero:

There is in fact a true law—namely, right reason—which is in accordance with nature, applies to all men, and is unchangeable and eternal. By its commands this law summons men to the performance of their duties; by its prohibitions it restrains them from doing wrong. Its commands and prohibitions always influence good men, but are without effect upon the bad. To invalidate this law by human legislation is never morally right, nor is it permissible ever to restrict its operation, and to annul it wholly is impossible. Neither the senate nor the people can absolve us from our obligation to obey this law, and it requires no Sextus Aelius to expound and interpret it. It will not lay down one rule at Rome and another at Athens, nor will it be one rule today and another tomorrow. But there will be one law, eternal and unchangeable, binding at all times upon all peoples; and there will be, as it were, one common master and ruler of men, namely God, who is the author of this law, its interpreter, and its sponsor. The man who will not obey it will abandon his better self, and, in denying the true nature of a man, will thereby suffer the severest of penalties, though he has escaped all the other consequences which men call punishment.[19]

In closing let me make two brief statements just to relate our subject to our times:

1. The general criticism directed by the modern positivists against Natural Law is that it is merely a part of ethics or ivory-tower idealism and has no place or part in the practical administration of law. It is my conviction, based on fourteen years of judicial service in the U.S. District Courts, that such criticism is entirely unfounded and untrue. In every court where justice is the aim, Natural Law is a definite part of the judicial process. It should not be scoffed at but studied and practiced.

2. In a notable book just published, Herbert Agar, the distinguished editor, author, social philosopher, and true American, offers some fine counsel for our critical and tragic times. One reviewer says of the book: "It is one of the best applications of an argument as old as the prophet Isaiah, to the conditions of the middle twentieth century to appear from an American pen." It is entitled *A Declaration of Faith.*

Mr. Agar declares his faith in law, not the law made by human tribunals or dictators and backed by force, but the Law of Nature which works in the conscience, demanding that men be just and compassionate. In an interesting chapter he traces the history of this concept of Natural Law, from its emergence in ancient Greece. For him Natural Law, permeating human society and setting it off from the society of the beasts, is discovered by reason. Mr. Agar sums up his position with a quotation from Goldwin Smith: "Justice has been justice, mercy has been mercy, honour has been honour, good faith has been good faith, truthfulness has been truthfulness from the beginning." These time-worn ideas and objective standards are the basis of the Natural Law which elevates human society above that of the beasts.

1. Sabine, A History of Political Theory, Chapter VIII (Rev. ed. 1950).
2. Manion, "The Natural Law Philosophy of the Founding Fathers," in University of Notre Dame Natural Law Institute Proceedings I (1949).
3. Baker, Sulla the Fortunate, Chapter II (1927).
4. Ibid., 279.
5. Ibid., 135, 137.
6. Ibid., 69.
7. Cambridge Ancient History, IX, 843 (1932).
8. Ibid., 305, 867.
9. Ibid., 862.
10. Ibid., 842.
11. Rommen, The Natural Law 19-20 (Tr. by Hanley 1948).
12. Ibid., 22.
13. Jeans, The Mysterious Universe 186 (Rev. ed. 1932).
14. Sabine, op. cit supra n. 1, at 149.
15. Quoted in Sabine, op. cit., at 148.
16. Baker, op. cit. supra n. 3, at 151, 152.
17. Citations to Cicero's comments pertaining to Natural Law may be found in Levy, "Natural Law in the Roman Period," in University of Notre Dame Natural Law Institute Proceedings II (1949).
18. Wilkin, Eternal Lawyer: A Legal Biography of Cicero, Chapter VIII (1947).
19. Sabine, op. cit., 164.

ST. THOMAS AQUINAS AND
THE NATURAL LAW

Thomas E. Davitt

IN attempting to understand the meaning of Natural
Law for St. Thomas Aquinas, it may be well at the very
outset to determine as clearly as possible, and as briefly
as seems advisable, what he means by "law" and what
he means by "natural." Then, having grasped the significance of these, perhaps we shall be better able to
understand Natural Law itself.

"Law"

Aquinas' approach to the meaning of law in general
is by way of an analysis of an ordinary man-made law,
say a law in regard to murder or stealing or taxes.
Such a law is a rule or measure of human actions.[1]
However, Aquinas does not stop with this merely
descriptive and somewhat superficial analysis of law.
To say that a thing is a rule does not at all tell what the
thing is in itself. Many different things may serve as a
rule or norm. Hence Aquinas proceeds further in his
attempt to determine what it is about a law that is
the basis for calling it a rule of action. What he is
seeking is the nature or essence of law.

Is this rule of action merely the words — oral or
written — through which the law is made known? Or
is it something that is expressed by these words?
Since words are used by men as a means of communi-

cation, the words of a law must be merely the expression of something that is in the mind of the lawmaker. What could this be in the mind of the lawmaker which is the very essence of law?

It is at this point that St. Thomas' examination of law becomes more penetrating. Let us take the example of a speed law — a modern example, it is true, but one that may help us to follow more readily his analysis — although the example of any law would serve the same purpose.

A speed law is concerned with promoting an aspect of the common good, namely, safe driving conditions. It does this by specifying a maximum speed — for instance, forty miles per hour — that is conducive to this end. There is a relation between this maximum speed and safety. This can even be demonstrated by conducting tests, say, on curves. The sharpness and bank of a curve together with the construction of an automobile will determine the maximum speed at which a car can successfully negotiate the curve — regardless of who drives the car or of how fast the driver may think he can go on this particular curve.

In other words, there is a factual relation between a certain maximum speed at which·an automobile may be driven and safe driving conditions. One is by its very nature *ordered* to the other. Observing the maximum speed is the means of bringing about safety. It is this order of means to end that the lawmakers must ascertain, as accurately as possible, if the law is going to meet the needs of a particular situation. Sane people will not accept an arbitrary speed law. The starting point, then, for the deliberations and evaluations of lawmakers is the *order* that actually exists between certain means and the end that the lawmakers wish to bring about.

When the lawmakers, after deliberating on the reports, let us say in this instance, of traffic engineers and the like, have judged that a certain maximum speed will accomplish their purpose, then it is this means ordered to safety that is chosen by them. This will be the content of the law.[2]

Finally, then, the lawmakers judge that this is the order of means to end that must be observed by the people. It is this *directive judgment* in the minds of the lawmakers — "This speed limit must be observed" — that is law. And since the essence of this judgment is the order of means to end that has been decided upon, law is also properly termed an *ordering*. Understood in this sense (and not as an expression of the will of the sovereign in the sense of Austin), it may also be called a *command*.[3] Law then for Aquinas is an ordering, in the minds of those in authority, of means necessary for the common good.[4]

It is this ordering, command, or directive judgment that is then promulgated to the people by the use of words — oral or written. Obviously, the people cannot be directed and obliged by a law until it is made known to them. Hence the promulgation of a law is the making known of the directive judgment that is in the mind of a lawmaker.[5] This, then, very briefly, is the basic meaning of law in Aquinas.

"Natural"

What does "natural" mean? "Natural," of course, refers to "nature" and just as in the case of law, so also in regard to nature, the approach is by way of an examination of observable phenomena. Nature, for Aquinas, is that which makes a thing to be what it is.[6] It is that which gives internal structure to a thing and that on account of which a thing has particular characteristics. A rose is not a bluebonnet, and that which determines the difference is the nature of the rose and the nature of the bluebonnet, expressing itself as the directing bio-principle of growth and development.

This expression manifests itself through dynamic inclinations or drives.[7] These inclinations or drives are both for the highest development of which the being is capable and for those things that are needed as a means of attaining this development. Thus the rosebush has an over-all master drive to produce roses. This is the highest development it is capable of. This is its purpose and its perfection. Any other plant can bring forth leaves, but only a rosebush can produce a rose. For a rosebush is internally structured to produce roses. No amount of experimental gardening or wishful thinking can make a rosebush bring forth bluebonnets or figs. No, a rosebush "naturally" produces roses. And when a rosebush does function properly so as to produce roses, it is called a "good" rosebush. Likewise, the rosebush has dynamic inclinations for those things that are necessary if it is to produce roses. It has a drive, for instance, to preserve itself in existence by seeking water through its roots and sunshine through its leaves. These are "good" for the rosebush. The word "natural," then, refers to the nature of a thing expressing itself through its dynamic inclinations or drives. So much for the meaning of "natural."

We now have examined briefly the meaning of "law" and the meaning of "natural" for Aquinas: law being an ordering in the minds of those with lawmaking authority, and natural referring to the nature of a thing and the dynamic inclinations that are expressed by it. Hence, if "Natural Law" is to have a meaning consistent with these facts, then the drives manifested by a man's nature must somehow connote such an ordering.

Natural Law

Aquinas' approach to Natural Law is, then, by way of a man's *basic drives or inclinations*. These are the observable phenomena upon which he centers his investigation. It is in these that he finds evidence of an ordering, by one in authority, of means necessary for the common good and, therefore, a law.

Let us see how this is true. The first basic inclination or drive that Aquinas examines in seeking an ordering of means to end is the master drive — that a man has in common with all beings, for instance, with the rose-bush — to reach the highest development of which he is capable, that is, to seek the attainment of his perfection. This is the same as seeking his highest good, since the good is that which perfects. Or to put it in terms of satisfaction, this is the drive that every man has to be happy. Precisely in what a man's highest possible development consists is not clear from this inclination alone. It has to be more completely determined from other sources. But it is obvious that a man's unique perfection, like that of all other beings, must consist in an attainment that pertains somehow to his greatest powers, and these are his intellect and will.

The second basic inclination — or rather group of inclinations — that Aquinas examines has to do with the prime requisite of a man's pursuit of perfection, and that is that he exist. Unless men exist they cannot advance toward their perfection. So, a man has a basic drive — in common with all beings — to preserve himself in existence. However, not only must the individual man preserve himself, but the human race itself must be preserved if men in general are to perfect themselves. Hence, a man has a basic inclination — in common with all animals — to unite sexually. But a man, being endowed with intellect and will, is essentially different from animals. He depends upon other men for the fulfilment of many of his needs. So he has a basic inclination to live in community with other men, which, as we shall note later, has a relation to property claims. Living together in community is, therefore, as far as Aquinas is concerned, a natural state for men consequent upon their basic inclination to do so. Further, since a man is endowed with intellect and will and has a unique purpose to accomplish, he must use his powers of knowing, judging, reasoning, and freely deciding or choosing in order that he may attain this destiny. Hence a man has a basic drive to use his intellectual and volitional powers. Every man's desire and urge to acquire knowledge and to make his own decisions is a manifestation of this drive.[8]

But how is there any indication of an ordering of a means to a common good in these basic drives of a man? Upon examination, it will be found that these inclinations, while promoting the existence and development of the individual person, by that very fact also promote the existence or development of the human community. And the human community, with all of its material and spiritual resources, is a common good which is communicable to many and in which

all of us participate. Hence there is in the basic inclination an indication of an ordering of means to a common good. Self-preservation, sexual union, living in
community, and use of the intellectual and volitional
powers are all means of bringing about the common
good of the human community.[9]

Before proceeding to the possibility of another and
higher common good to which the basic inclinations
may be ordered, let us examine whether or not the
order we have already discerned (of means to a common good) is the result of a previous ordering in the
mind of someone in authority. For law, as we saw,
must originate from one in authority. In other words,
what is the cause of this order observable in a man's
inclinations?

Chance may perhaps be a sufficient explanation of
simple and unrepeated order. But if the order is complex and recurrent, then some cause more adequate is
demanded by the human mind. At least, this is the way
the human mind operates when it daily attributes
causes to the ever recurring manifestations of order
that it encounters.

The cause, however, that adequately explains order
must be an intellectual one. Order implies a relation
between two things and only an intellect can perceive a relation, especially — as is the case in law —
when neither term of the relation is as yet an objective
reality: for instance, the safe driving conditions which
the legislator envisions and the observance of a certain
speed limit which he plans on enacting into a law. But
no man has caused the order in any other man's nature
and inclinations. Hence the intellectual being that
caused this order must be extratemporal, transmun-
dane, suprahuman.[10] It is here that the order observ-

able in a man's basic inclinations begins to appear in clear and sharp perspective. It is now identifiable as an expression of an ordering that pre-existed in the intellect of the Supreme Orderer.[11] If this is true, then St. Thomas is well on his way to finding in a man's basic inclinations the expression of a very real law.

But how is the Supreme Orderer in a position of authority? He has given existence to the order observable in a man's nature and inclinations. As a consequence, a man has no choice about the fact that he is made the way he is, that he is what he is with certain basic drives. These drives demand a definite way of acting, and hence a man is subject to their direction. In being subject to them, he is subject to the one who caused them. And since the correlative of "subjection to" is "authority over," the one who caused these directives has authority over a man who is subject to them. Therefore the ordering expressed by a man's basic inclinations derives from one with authority.[12]

The common good of the human community, however, is not the only common good to which the ordering expressed by the inclinations is directed. There is a higher and final common good in relation to which the common good of the human community is itself only a means. And it is in the master inclination for the highest development of which a man is capable that the clue to this fact may be found. This master inclination is, as we have noted, for those things that will bring about a man's perfection. It is for the good itself, since to seek what is truly good for a man is to seek what will perfect him. But what will ultimately perfect a man is the possession of all good, otherwise his full potentialities will never be realized. All good, however, is to be found only in its source — the Creator.

If, however, the Creator is the ultimate and complete good which is communicable to many through their individual possession of Him, then He is also the common good of all men. Hence the ultimate common good which is the end of this primordial ordering is the Creator himself.[13]

Therefore the observable phenomenon of a man's basic inclinations manifesting order is an expression of a law. This law is an ordering in the mind of one with authority and it is for the common good.

The promulgation of this law, then, is the very phenomenon we have been analyzing: the order observable in the basic drives of a man. For law is known from its promulgation.

Hence this ordering in the mind of the Eternal Lawmaker is called by St. Thomas the *Eternal Law*. Its promulgation through man's natural inclinations is the *Natural Law*. Therefore, looked at from the standpoint of the law which they express, a man's basic inclinations represent so many demands of the Eternal Law. Hence the Natural Law is really the demands of the Eternal Law as expressed by a man's basic drives or inclinations.

HOW NATURAL LAW IS KNOWN

How does a man know these inclinations or drives, and what is the extent of the knowledge that he acquires from them?

Since a man is an intellectual being, he is aware of these inclinations and their object or end. He knows, for instance, that he has a drive or inclination to preserve himself in existence, and the like. So he *connaturally* — that is, without any reasoning — judges that all those things to which he has a natural inclination are good and ought to be sought after and that their contraries are bad and should be avoided. Therefore his elementary judgments as to what is good and bad follow from the knowledge of his inclinations.

Hence, after judging that he should strive to attain his perfection (or to put it in other ways, as we have, that he should do what is good or that he should seek happiness) and that he should avoid what is not conducive to this end, he forms the following judgments as to what some of the basic things are that are a necessary means to this end. He judges that it is good to preserve himself in existence and that not to do so, by suicide for instance, is evil; he judges that it is good to unite sexually and that not to unite sexually is bad; he judges that it is good and not evil to live with other men in community and that living apart from them is bad; he judges that it is good to use his intellectual and volitional powers and that not to do so is evil.[14] And since he perceives as immediately evident those things that are necessarily connected with these judgments and without which the purpose of the inclinations themselves would be nullified, he judges that the haphazard, random, and arbitrary killing of other men, sexual union, and the use of external things and of his own mental powers is bad. On the contrary, he judges that the carrying on of these activities according to some distinction and restrictions — even according to some elementary pattern — is good and the thing to be done: not everyone is to be killed at random; sexual union may not be had promiscuously with any and every one; what is "thine" is distinct from what is "mine" and may not be claimed or used indiscriminately (which is the basis for distinguishing between justice and injustice in regard to property); and a man's mental powers are not to be used indifferently and casually, but in a manner that sooner or later will lead to a consideration of the purpose of living and the means that must be employed to accomplish it.[15] The presence of these elementary judgments in men is fully attested to, if one is interested, by the extensive research of anthropology. The full importance and impact of these elementary judgments on our lives can be better realized if we try to imagine for a moment what life would be like if their opposites were true: if men judged — and acted accordingly — that it is evil to preserve one's life; that sexual union is evil; that living with other men in community is evil; and that the use of one's mental powers is evil. Such living would be the very opposite of what we now know as human and rational. For, when a man does act this way, we call him irrational and insane and remove him from social living.

So, if it be asked what is the extent of the demands known from the inclinations, the answer would be: that which is contained in these few — rather than many — judgments just mentioned. Hence, according to this analysis, the Natural Law could be defined as: *the elementary demands expressed by a man's basic inclinations which are known connaturally.*

DOES NATURAL LAW CHANGE?

And now another important question presents itself: Do these inclinations and judgments that we have been examining change? In other words, does the Natural Law change?

This question cannot be answered with a simple no or yes. In the first place, as far as the basic inclinations themselves are concerned, they do not change.[16] Every man who is normal has these inclinations. However, in regard to the judgments that are formed consequent upon these inclinations, a distinction has to be made. Concerning the master inclination to seek perfection and the inclination to use one's mental powers, the judgment that it is good rather than bad to do so does not change. But the judgments in regard to the other inclinations may vary in one of two ways. First, although the inclinations to preserve one's life, unite sexually, and live in society remain the same, the judgment that a man makes in regard to them may be influenced by environment, education, or vicious habits.[17] As a consequence, his reasoning may be directed by false principles. Thus, even though a man has an inclination to preserve his own life, he may, because of education and environment, judge that suicide is good and join a suicide cult. His judgment then is contrary to his natural inclination. To be noted, however, is the fact that, even though he has maneuvered himself into judging that it is good not to preserve his life, nevertheless his natural inclination to do so still persists. Consequently, he is compelled to struggle against the inclination, to some degree at least, before he can bring himself to end his life by his own hand. And when these unfortunate instances occur, we are always ready to say that perhaps the victim was deranged.

The second way that the judgments a man makes according to his inclinations may vary, is when the inclinations themselves demand it.[18] This follows from the very dynamic of the inclination to use the intellectual power of knowing, judging, reasoning, and freely deciding or choosing. For instance, a man judges that the preservation of his own life is good and to be secured at all costs. Does it follow from this that he should not volunteer to give his life, if need be, in defense of his country? Not if the drive demanding that he use his power of reasoning means anything. For in this situation there are two goods to be weighed and evaluated: his continued existence and the community's continued existence. And since the existence of the community is a greater good than the existence of the individual[19] (for, among other reasons, other individuals without the community could not survive), it should be judged to be of greater value. Hence it is the inclinations themselves taken *in toto* that demand that the judgment that it is good to preserve one's life give place in this instance to another judgment — reached after much reasoning — that it is better to give one's life.

Again, however, it may be well to note that even in the case of a man judging that it is good to give his life for his country and actually doing so, his drive to preserve his own life still persists. And it is the persistence of this inclination that makes his final action heroic. He has accomplished something that was, in one sense, contrary to one of the deepest demands expressed by his nature, but he has done it on account of a higher cause.

It is to be noted, of course, that what we have just been observing in regard to variations of judgment concerning self-preservation is, in like manner, true also of judgments concerning sexual union and living in community.

NATURAL LAW AND REVEALED LAW

Such, then, in brief outline, is St. Thomas' idea of the Natural Law. It is a *law* inasmuch as it is a promulgation of an ordering in the mind of the Supreme Law-maker. It is *natural* insofar as this promulgation takes place through the inclinations or drives that are a dynamic expression of every man's nature.

Hence at this point a somewhat prevalent misconception of St. Thomas' concept of the Natural Law may well be pointed out. Many seem to have the impression that the Natural Law refers to certain basic truths that may be known either from the use of reason *or from revelation*.[20] Revelation is here taken to mean, for instance, the Ten Commandments. While it may be true that there is a coincidence between the content of the commands known by faith in the authority of Sacred Scripture and the demands of a man's basic inclinations known connaturally, nevertheless this coincidence is entirely beyond any consideration of the Natural Law as such. If the word "natural" means anything at all, it refers to the nature of a man, and when used with "law," "natural" must refer to an ordering that is manifested in the inclinations of a man's nature and to nothing else. Hence, taken in itself, there is nothing religious or theological in the "Natural Law" of Aquinas — if by religion and theology are meant truths to which the mind assents because of the authority of the word of God as revealed in the Sacred Scriptures. If it is based on this kind of revelation, then Natural Law is not natural; it is supernatural. No, the truths of the Natural Law are assented to by the human mind simply because of the evidence that is observable in a man's natural inclinations: the evidence of an ordering that ultimately is recognized as a law. That is why numerous men — from Plato, Aristotle, and Cicero on down to Hooker, Grotius, Locke, Vattel, Burlamaqui, Stammler, and many others — could hold "Natural Law" without its being related to religious faith. The fact that Aquinas may treat such questions as "Natural Law" within a theological framework, as he does at times, has no bearing on this particular point. The validity of his conclusions in regard to a law expressed in man's nature — like his conclusions in regard to any other natural phenomena—rests squarely on the observable evidence that is available to all. As a matter of fact, it is only through an examination and interpretation of the natural that a man can grasp the meaning of the supernatural.

NATURAL LAW: THE COMPASS

There is also another misconception of the Natural Law that it may be profitable to mention at this time. From what we have observed of the Natural Law, it is obvious that it gives, and is intended to give, only elementary directives. But, again, many seem to be laboring under the impression that the Natural Law is supposed to furnish ready-made solutions for whatever detailed problems of justice may arise, for instance, in torts or crimes.[21] It is thought that by a simple process of deduction, Natural Law furnishes the appropriate answer. Nothing could be farther from the truth. The relation of Natural Law to the man-made law of legislation and adjudication is similar to the relation of a compass to navigation. A compass indicates basic directions, but it will not navigate. Only a man skilled in navigation and using the basic directives furnished by a compass can do that. For instance, in regard to the speed law we examined above, will Natural Law of itself indicate whether the speed limit should be 30 mph, 50 mph, or 40 mph? Of course not. This may have to be determined, as we said, even by conducting traffic tests. Then of what value is Natural Law? Its importance becomes evident if one asks and answers certain questions pertinent to any legislation or adjudication. Why have a speed law? To bring about conditions of safety. But why bring about conditions of safety? To preserve human life. Why preserve human life? Because it is a demand of a man's nature and hence not to do so would be evil. This is the basic directive of a man's nature — the compass.

Hence a lawmaker must use his power of reasoning in determining how the elementary directives contained in a man's basic drives may be implemented in the numberless situations that arise every day. He must reason both deductively and inductively — that is, he must seek conclusions insofar as they follow from premises he already knows (whether these be from other sciences, or from precedent, or from other legislation including ethical and religious), or insofar as they follow from diversified tests and experiments.[22] From the fact that crime in general should be punished, a lawmaker may conclude that murder should be punished. But whether it should be punished by ten, twenty, or thirty years imprisonment may have to be determined by a careful examination and detailed study of the deterrent effect that such prison sentences have had on the criminal element in the community in recent years.

In this manner legislators and judges give specific determination to the general directives of Natural Law. If it should be said that, if this is the case, then Natural Law really is not of much help in solving practical problems, it can only be answered that neither is a compass of much help in solving problems of navigation — unless one realizes that without a compass navigation is aimless and meaningless, while with it navigation has purpose and significance.

Again, upon hearing of St. Thomas' explanation of the Natural Law, some may say that it contains nothing that is not already evident — that it is good to preserve one's life, that there is a difference between justice and injustice, and the other judgments mentioned above. Well, that is as it should be. If men connaturally form the judgments that Aquinas says they do, then — unless their judgments have been affected in the manner already mentioned — it is only to be expected that they would speak of these things as evident.

For this reason, attempts to deny the reality of Natural Law in Aquinas' sense have produced some paradoxical results. These attempts, for the most part, are like the efforts of the man we have all heard about who bought a new boomerang and then spent the rest of his life trying to throw away his old one. After a man has rejected Natural Law as outmoded or useless, it inevitably reasserts itself in his thinking and speaking. That good should be distinguished from bad, right from wrong, justice from injustice, that acts promoting health and safety and the like are good, that acts like murder and stealing are evil, these all make their appearance now as some sort of assumed axioms. They may be called "jural postulates,"[23] or "self-assertion" assumptions,[24] or "substantial justice," or even self-evident "fundamental principles of law."[25] What has occurred here is not that Natural Law in St. Thomas' sense has been rejected, since these postulates and assumptions are, for the most part, nothing but Natural

Law judgments. What has been rejected is a misconception of Aquinas' explanation of the Natural Law and a conception of Natural Law more like that of later authors.

NATURAL LAW AND LAWYERS' LAW

What are some of the implications of Natural Law as understood by Aquinas in regard to man-made legislation or adjudication? Does it mean more emphasis on those aspects of "lawyers' law" that favor the individual or on those aspects that may be termed sociological?

From what we have been observing throughout this paper, it should be obvious that, in one sense, Natural Law underlies, or well could underlie, either trend. Natural Law is so basic and operates at such a profound level that, as long as its demands are recognized, it may well be present — depending on conditions — in either development.

But there are certain broad consequences that do affect the familiar areas of law. In constitutional law, certain claims or "rights" that are referred to as "fundamental" and "inalienable" are precisely that — fundamental and inalienable. They are founded on the demands expressed by a man's nature. Many of the rights protected by "due process" would not vary with future judicial decisions that might be based on experimental pragmatism. In crimes, as far as "mens rea" is concerned, since a man has dominion over his actions by his power of free decision, he is primarily responsible for his crime. True, there are other factors, including social ones, that have their influence on the criminal. But as long as he is free to decide whether he will or will not commit crime, his responsibility is primary and that of society — while most important — is secondary. In torts, the relations between the individual person and society are equally, if not more, complex. The interrelationships between proper and common goods and interests must ever be kept in balance. But even here liability in the true sense must follow its only possible source — freedom to do or not to do the action in question. Hence, again, liability must be centered primarily in the individual person, and secondarily in others united in society. St. Thomas would certainly agree that the morals of social liability ". . . are those of Robin Hood . . . "[26] Concerning property, the basic claim or "right" to ownership derives directly from a demand expressed by man's nature — a demand based on the distinction of "mine" from "thine" and the relation to "mine" of a man's unique ability to elaborate material things by giving them new form and, therefore, added value.[27] This is the basis of the labor contract. Finally, in equity Natural Law finds its finest witness. In calling, if need be, upon principles that are beyond statutes and precedent, equity has always testified to the reality and importance of Natural Law. For Aquinas, as for countless other legal thinkers, Natural Law as operative in equity is the last recourse of justice.

Consequences

From these brief and all too inadequate remarks, perhaps some idea may be got of what the Natural Law means for St. Thomas and what some of its practical implications are. As is clear, his whole concept of Natural Law — based as it is on the ideas of nature and law — presupposes his interpretation of what a man is and what existence means. Because this interpretation was clear-cut and exact, it served as an instrument by means of which he could refine the concept of law into its basic and essential elements. His predecessors, such as Plato, Aristotle, and Cicero, did not have such an instrument and hence their concept of law was formulated in terms of a description of law and not of its essence, as Aquinas' was.

And many of Aquinas' successors, since they have not held this interpretation, have had a tendency to overstate what can be known of justice and injustice merely by a process of rational deduction. The consequence of this has been that there are those who think that "Natural Law" pretends to be some sort of magic formula that furnishes handy answers for whatever practical legal questions may arise. And upon realizing the obvious, namely, that such a pretension is absurd, they close their minds to the possibility of a more basic and valid meaning of Natural Law, which must, under some guise, be assumed as a basis of any legal thinking — a fact to which we have already alluded. It would seem that it was the "Natural Law" theories of such men as Grotius, Pufendorf, Locke, and others, rather than that of Aquinas, that may have given rise to this ill-founded and overextended notion of "Natural Law."[28] For, besides the fact of what these men wrote, there is the other fact that their writings have been more widely read and better understood in legal circles than Aquinas'. This could not help but produce the result that it has.

Finally, we might observe that, if an idea reoccurs in the history of legal thought as persistently as "Natural Law" does and if at the same time this idea is expressed under so many different forms and developed in so many diversified ways, then it seems that there is only one conclusion that can be drawn from these facts: there must be some definite reality that men are trying to explain and this reality is of its nature intricate and complex. If this is the case, then we have pointed up for us, not only the importance, but also the necessity of a proper interpretation of this reality as a prelude to legal thinking. If legal thinking is to be other than superficial, this is certainly one of its prerequisites.

And it seems only too true today that not a few legal minds, since they profess to follow no compass, may have lost their legal bearings and are foundering and awash in mountainous seas of uncertainty. Perhaps a rescue can be effected, but only if it is realized that there is a destination to be reached and that a compass and directions are needed in order to reach it. Otherwise, what difference does it make if a man is lost? For the man, however, who would seek to know this destination and to receive help in plotting the course of life and law accordingly, there is a chart available in the writings of St. Thomas Aquinas. He was one of the great minds of all times, and his work on the meaning of law — the first treatise of its kind — is recognized more and more by those who study it seriously, as being in its main outlines as valid today as it was the day it was written.[29]

1. Aquinas, 1-2 Summa Theologiae 90, 1.
2. Aquinas, 2-2 *op. cit.* 47.
3. Aquinas, 1-2 *op cit.* 17, 1.
4. *Ibid,* 90, 4.
5. *Ibid.*
6. Aquinas, 1 *op. cit.* 29, 2, 3, and 39, 2, 3.
7. Aquinas, 1 *op. cit.* 80, 1 and 1-2, 8, 1.
8. Aquinas, 1-2, *op. cit.* 94, 2.

9. Aquinas, 1 *op. cit* 65, 2; 3 Contra Gentiles 80.
10. Aquinas, 1 Sum. Theol. 2, 3.
11. Aquinas, 1-2 *op. cit.* 93.
12. *Loc. cit.*
13. Aquinas, 1 *op. cit.* 65, 2.
14. Aquinas, 1-2 *op. cit.* 94, 2.
15. *Loc. cit.* and 100, 1. On Connatural Knowledge see Maritain, Man and the State 89 (1951).
16. Aquinas, 1-2 *op. cit.* 94, 4.
17. *Ibid.* 93, 6.
18. *Ibid.* 94, 5.
19. Aquinas, 3 Contra Gentiles 69.
20. See for instance, 13 Ohio St. L. J. 162, 170 (1951).
21. For an example of this in a recent work, see Pound, Justice According to Law 15, 28 (1951).
22. Aquinas, 1-2 Sum. Theol. 95, 2.
23. Pound, An Introduction to the Philosophy of Law. 169, 192 (1922) and Social Control Through Law 81, 113 (1942).
24. Von Ihering, Law as a Means to an End 47, 59 (1924).
25. Mr. Justice Holmes in McDonald v. Mabee, 243 U.S. 90, 92 (1917) and Lochner v. New York, 198 U.S. 45, 46 (1905).
26. Pound, Justice According to Law 14 (1951).
27. For a development of this point, see Maritain, Freedom in the Modern World 193 (1936).
28. See for instance, Locke's statement in An Essay Concerning Human Understanding, Bk. III, c. 11, n. 16; Bk. IV, c. 3, n. 18-20 (1714).
29. Worth noting is Von Ihering's remark that if he had known St. Thomas before he wrote his book, without doubt he would not have written it. "The fundamental ideas which I have set forth have already been expressed by this powerful thinker with perfect clarity and in a striking manner." Der Zweck im Recht, 2nd ed. t. II, p. 161, n. 2 (translation mine).

RICHARD HOOKER AND THE
ORIGINS OF AMERICAN
CONSTITUTIONALISM

John S. Marshall

RICHARD Hooker, one of the greatest of the
Elizabethans, is usually thought of either as a distinguished writer of magnificent prose or as the most
illustrious of Anglican theologians. Not so often is he
considered as a legal theorist, as the one who synthe-
sized medieval law with the new nationalism and
thus saved much of the medieval legal heritage for
us. He saved it for us by interpreting it in the light
of later English legal history, Roman law, and Aristotle.

We can hardly appreciate his contribution to legal
thought unless we know that he was for six years the
Master of the Temple. While there, he was in constant
conversation with the lawyers and students of the
Inns of Court, and through such contacts he came to
formulate the conception of his *Polity*. As we read him
we find that the whole of English political history was
before his mind from the Conquest to Henry VIII and
Elizabeth I. To interpret this he used not only English
common law but Roman law, Canon law, the Acts of
Supremacy, and Aristotle's *Politics*. The result was the
legal conceptions of the first and eighth books of the
Ecclesiastical Polity. As Houk says, "Hooker might have
prevented some misunderstanding had he entitled his
work *Of the Laws of Ecclesiastical and Civil Polity*."[1]

To understand the contribution of Richard Hooker we must realize that he was thinking in terms of the legal problems of the time, and that he was helping to crystallize the fluid legal thought of his age. Earlier, when the Tudor sovereigns needed new powers to administer the realm, there seemed a possibility that Roman law would be used for that purpose and that the liberties of the individual granted by the common law would be destroyed. But by the time of Hooker the common law was being defended by able lawyers, and Hooker sympathized with this tradition of the common law. Although the courts of chancery had threatened to form a league with those who would have destroyed the common law, in the end they did succeed, and in fact played an able part in saving the common law from its own limitations. Equity was used to mitigate the rigors of the common law, and this element from Roman law was proving to be a valuable aid in adjusting the older common law system to the new conditions of modern life. Equity was also accepted by Hooker, and he defended it as a broad aspect of legal reason, because it was the reasonableness of the law which was his theme.

The Acts of Supremacy had threatened the ancient constitutional liberties and were still threatening them. Yet the autonomy and complete sovereignty of the realm were being accepted as part of the legal heritage. It was Hooker's task to conceive the autonomous sovereign state in terms of the older monarchical constitution and its limitation of the royal power. The lawyers of the Inns of Court, as exponents of the common law, were attached to the older conception of the constitution. Although they desired the autonomy of the national state, they wished constitutional safeguards against the growing sovereignty of the monarch. It was this attempted synthesis of old and new which was Hooker's particular problem. It is not quite correct to say that Hooker is purely medieval. The legal conception of the *Polity* is primarily the revision of St. Thomas Aquinas in the light of medieval English law, Roman law, and the philosophy of Aristotle's *Politics*.

At the time that the lawyers were attempting to save the older law in a revised form, there came to the fore a group of reformers who desired the destruction of common law, equity, and the constitution. The English Calvinists desired a revolution which would completely destroy the ancient church and the ancient legal system. They wished to do in England what they later did in New England,[2] that is, destroy the ancient law, decisions in equity, and the ancient monarchical constitution. In their place they wished to set up the Mosaic law as the only legal code for the land. This code was to be administered literally and without judicial clemency. In other words, there could be no deviation from the code and no judge-made law. As Pound points out, the essentially Puritan mind dislikes judicial use of equity; the Calvinistic mind prefers strict adherence to the letter of the law.

Although the law courts during the reign of Elizabeth were administered much as they had been in the early part of the reign of Henry VIII, yet the reformers desired to remove what they considered to be the debris of the idolatrous Middle Ages. They were desirous of introducing a new order based not on man-made institutions but on God's own law for man, the law given on Sinai to Moses. Every feature of life should be regulated by the divine command, and this divine command is to be found in the biblical law. This was indeed a radical reformation of the legal system. It was a return to a very rudimentary and harsh ancient legal system. The Puritan knew nothing of the mitigation of the rigors of the Mosaic law through the interpretation of the Mishnah; and if he did know about it, he repudiated it as a destruction of God's own law through the process of man-made interpretation.

The Puritan was also unappreciative of the necessity for a constitutional limitation of power. In his fine enthusiasm for the democratic principles borrowed from Geneva, he assumed that popular sovereignty would of itself prevent tyranny. But the student of ancient law knows that such an assumption is naïve, because a popular government is quite as capable of tyranny as a monarchy or an aristocracy.

Hooker's task was the preservation of the medieval legal system. It is the ancient classical Christian conception of society, and the law of that society, which Hooker wished to preserve. In his *Ecclesiastical Polity* he is not defending a distinctly new form of church and state. He is specifically defending a modified form of the medieval order in both church and state. Whitehead thinks of Hooker as a "belated medievalist," one who does not understand the essentially modern conception of reason.[3] What Whitehead does not understand is that Hooker thinks as a lawyer. The reason which he defends is that of the medieval legal mind, and legal reason is just what he saved for us. In repudiating the claims of the Calvinists he drew upon all past wisdom: he drew from Bracton; he drew from St. Thomas; he drew from Justinian; he drew from Aristotle.

The Protestant Reformation had had an effect upon English thought. Hooker did not repudiate that influence, but he handled it in a legally judicial way. He treated the Protestant Reformation in its English form as a purification and modification of the older order; but he did not allow the destructive aspects of the Reformation to triumph. What he was doing was essentially saving the medieval law for the Anglo-Saxon world. In the extreme reformation planned by the Calvinists there was such an innovation as would have destroyed the whole legal system. If we examine the attack we shall see by contrast what Hooker was trying to preserve.

What was actually under attack was that kind of law which Hooker calls *the law of reason.* Being an Englishman, he considered the eternal law for man to be reasonable, and as Sir Frederick Pollock points out, *the law of nature* is hidden in English law under the notion of judicial wisdom. It is this fundamental appropriateness of certain laws to human life and its needs which he considers to be fundamental. This is the law embedded in creation by God's own act. This is the law which Moses might attempt to modify because of people's hardness of heart; and yet it is eternal in spite of the accommodation which Moses had to make. This law can be appealed to by the judge even though it was never passed by any legislature or asserted by any king. We must not fancy that Hooker thinks of the law of reason as did the radical thinkers of the seventeenth and eighteenth centuries. It is not an abstract law which can be asserted with such stark independence that it becomes the source of unhistoric revolutions. Rather, it is revealed in the long and empiric wisdom of judicial experience as the basic law of human life.

The law of creation is written in God's creatures and is presupposed in the biblical revelation. Hooker is amazed when the Bible is made a book of positive law without reference to historic experience. He is convinced that such biblical radicalism is morally dangerous. He considers biblical radicalism the source of a deadly immorality, an immorality based on the failure to realize that our obligations transcend specific requirements of biblical legislation.[4] The proposed legalism is unredeemed by any moral modification of the positive rigor of a rigidly enforced Mosaic system.

We can put this matter in another way, and say that Hooker is defending historic experience. He is defending the whole method of precedent as the source of legal development. Hooker understood that there is an ethical phase of our Anglo-Saxon law and that the method of judicial modification of traditional law is a way of redeeming society through a gradual moralization of what was previously less moral, or immoral.

This leads us to see with fresh eyes the point I mentioned before. The Puritan did not wish to save the individual from the rigors of the Mosaic law. Since the law was supposed to be divine, the full rigor of the law was desirable. Neither decisions in equity nor constitutional limitations should spare the individual from the wrath of God's law. The full force of the law was God's sharp punishment of evil. Even Charles II, and he was no gentle man, was amazed at the rigor of Massachusetts' legal enforcement. I am not an admirer of the Stuarts, but we should be grateful that the traditional law was brought to Boston by the hands of a Royal Stuart governor.

How Hooker Influenced the History of the Law

Hooker is one of the few really significant thinkers

who have influenced Anglo-American social history. Along with Bacon, Hobbes, and Locke, he is one of the few really creative minds of our history. A generation ago this would not have been admitted. For example, Henderson in his article on Hooker in the eleventh edition of the *Encyclopaedia Britannica* says that Hooker cannot rank with such of his contemporaries as Spenser, Bacon, and Shakespeare as a man of essential greatness.[5] Now such critical minds as Sir Ernest Barker and Sir Basil Wiley place him in the forefront of the history of English and American thought. Northrop even goes so far in his book, *The Meeting of East and West,* as to make Hooker the decisive English genius, the man who makes modern England different from the rest of the world.[6] This is to claim both too much and too little for Hooker. He is probably not the decisive genius of modern England, and he has more influence on American thought than we are aware of.

Hooker is one of those geniuses whose influence lies in a particular synthesis of diverse elements: his is an essentially Aristotelian genius. Aristotle himself brings together diverse elements into one synthesis. He is par excellence the synthesizer of human wisdom. Fr. Reginald Garrigou-Lagrange recognizes the synthetic element as the really distinctive quality of St. Thomas' thought; and he entitles an introduction to the theology of St. Thomas, *La Synthèse Thomiste,* the Thomistic Synthesis. Hooker is in the great tradition of Aristotle and St. Thomas. His contribution lies in the bringing together of many elements into one whole; and it is by this synthesis that he is to be judged.

Because Hooker gives us a synthesis, his name is not mentioned in legal history as often as are those of the numerous legal authorities who furnish the several elements of his total synthesis. If the names of these persons who express various aspects of the total synthesis are brought to our attention, then we realize how much we owe to Richard Hooker. But if the total synthesis had been lost, then it is doubtful whether these several legal authorities would have been historically as significant as they now are.

For example, Sir Edward Coke is in legal history the hero of the common law. It is he who with fanatic zeal defended this phase of our legal medieval heritage. It is he who reproved James I in terms of legal wisdom; he it was who defended reason as the wisdom of judicial precedent. This is a most distinctive element of the Hooker synthesis. Sir Edward knew Hooker and sat under Hooker's ministration when the judicious divine was Master of the Temple. Both Hooker and Coke learned from the common law the meaning of reason as the lawyer understands it. Hooker defended this reason as a part of the whole reason of God, the universe, and man. Sir Edward defended it in terms of the heritage of the common law. No well-trained legal thinker fails to realize the enormous influence of Coke's *Institutes* on early American decisions. Coke and Blackstone were the authorities who educated the developing legal minds of the early nineteenth century. It is Coke who probably made this nation the greatest common law nation of the modern world. Coke, the Elizabethan lawyer, is the one who defended the common law against the Stuarts and educated the American legal profession in the mysteries of the common law and legal reason.

Again, it is the decisions of the courts of chancery upon which modern Anglo-American equity is founded.

Equity also is an element of the Hooker synthesis. One of the institutions of freedom which really developed in the Elizabethan period was the Court of Chancery. Here the rigors of the common law were mitigated by decisions in equity. This development of legal procedure was highly satisfactory to Hooker.[7] To his mind equity was one of the necessary aspects of essential reasonableness. Without it the legal system lacked that corrective influence which was so necessary to make the law in application truly reasonable. The courts of equity express one aspect of that total legal synthesis which was Hooker's.

In Hooker's synthesis there is another element which is of equal importance. It is the constitution as a limitation of sovereignty; and it is fundamental to Hooker's thought. He had learned apparently from Bracton that it should be the law that makes the king.[8] This means that the king is king because he obtains his position through the constitution and rules under the constitution. The tradition of Bracton is the ancient English notion of the constitution. It is that notion which the Tudors weakened and which the Stuarts later tried to destroy. It is the ancient English constitution which Shakespeare loved and which Hooker defended.

The fathers of the American Revolution knew Hooker and quoted him. The authors of our Constitution did not quote Hooker, but they did work out the Constitution in terms which reflect the principles defended by Hooker, and which were mediated to them by Locke and Blackstone. Locke specifically tells us that his notion of the constitution was derived from Hooker. Blackstone, also in the tradition of Hooker, was always in the background when the American Constitution was written, and he was used in the interpretation of what the Constitution was meant to imply.

We must grant, of course, that there were seventeenth- and eighteenth-century elements in our Constitution unknown to Hooker. However, the concept of the limitation of sovereignty — that is, the law as supreme over the sovereign — is the constitutional notion stressed by Hooker and contributed directly by him to Locke and Blackstone. If we conceive the Constitution in broad terms, and are — as good legal theorists — loose constructionists, we see that the Constitution as interpreted by the Supreme Court takes on the character of Blackstone and Coke. In the hands of Chief Justice Marshall and his successors, the Constitution proves to be more and more a document which is essentially an expression of Edward Coke and Blackstone. It is an expression of the essential limitations of power through general limitation of sovereignty, and the interpretation of all legislation through judicial wisdom. The Constitution in its broadest sense is the modification of sovereignty by judicial wisdom. This is indeed the very spirit of Hooker.

Perhaps we should elaborate this thesis somewhat further. The Constitution of the United States as it left the hands of the convention which composed it was a document which presented the fundamental law of the land as formal and explicit. It was influenced by the school of thought which interpreted the law of nature as an obvious set of principles. The French school of Natural Law reflected the seventeenth-century notion that legal wisdom could be reduced to a very simple set of self-evident propositions. It is this sort of a notion which prevails in the American Declaration of Independence, and there is a good deal of it in the

Federalist. Our Constitutional Convention did not mean to carry this type of thinking to a most extreme length; still it was fundamentally influenced by the abstract conception of the law of nature then dominant on the Continent.

However, the American legal mind had been trained in the common law and in the general scheme of English constitutional principles. When the Constitution was put into operation and was interpreted by the Supreme Court, then its meaning was expressed in forms which embodied the traditional English scheme. And mind you, the tendency of the American legal mind was to use the older legal tradition. It was the conservative Blackstone and the highly traditional Coke who were popular. It was Hooker's kind of legal reasoning which the Supreme Court of the United States used in interpreting its Constitution. If we accept the principle that the Constitution is what it is interpreted by the courts to be, the Constitution is a legal system which embodies the limitation of sovereignty through those safeguards of liberty of which Hooker was the exponent.

Hooker's Conception of the Constitution

Before we approach Hooker's conception of the constitution it is necessary to make clear the status of the eighth book of the *Polity.* As has been true of so many great men, Hooker's writings have been the object of constant party strife. That is a testimony to his essential greatness. Many parties have desired his influence and have debated the authenticity of part of his writings. The first five books of the *Polity* were published under Hooker's own supervision; and therefore about them there can be no serious question. The last three books, however, remained unpublished when he died, and did not appear in that generation. The rumor was that Mrs. Hooker had allowed certain Puritan ministers to destroy the completed manuscripts and that only certain imperfect drafts remained.

Only in 1648, forty-eight years after Hooker's death, was the eighth book published. It undoubtedly teaches a constitutional view which is alien to that of the patriarchal conception of the divine right of kings. As Hooker was considered to be the exponent of the truly Anglican conception of church and state, the constitutionalism of the eighth book was undoubtedly an embarrassment to the High Royalist party. Their position is expressed in literary form in the life of Hooker written by Izaak Walton, where we are told that the eighth book was changed by the Puritans.

The truth of this whole matter has been made explicit by the recent researches of Professor C. J. Sisson.[9] Internal evidence should have convinced us long ago that the political conceptions of the eighth book are identical with those of the first book. The first book is as clearly constitutional as the eighth. Richard Baxter pointed that out in the seventeenth century,[10] and Houk did the same in 1930.[11] Sisson, however, has proved the same thing by external evidence. He examined the records of the court of chancery about the Hooker estate. There it is made clear that Mrs. Hooker was not the irresponsible person that Walton says she was. Apparently the Hooker manuscripts were not published because the days were not appropriate for their appearance. They were too openly constitutional for the times of James I; and they could only appear when the possibility of a limited monarchy was at hand.

They were published at a time when the constitutional conception was being revised, and they were used by Locke in his defense of constitutional government. The truth seems to be that Hooker never did finish the last three books. What we have is the incomplete form of what was to have been his exposition of constitutional government.

Like Aristotle, Hooker believes that the character of the state is determined by its constitution. He differs from Aristotle, however, in making the state more of a construction than does the Stagirite. But the state, although to some extent a construction, is a corporation, something that does not die. The healthy state is something perpetual and normally indissoluble. Hooker's notion is that of a constitutional lawyer, for he does believe that artifice and construction go into the making of the state. Yet the result is a permanent and real entity; it is a national personality.

The constitution is important because it gives its character to the national state — because it makes the national reality what it is. Of course, the constitution is not conceived simply as a document of a very simple body of laws. It is the center of that organic set of laws which express the way of life of the corporate body. If the fundamental constitution is changed, then the national personality is also changed, because the personality of the national life is to be found in its constitution.

This notion of Hooker, this stress on the constitution, is a conception that has become a part of the American heritage. It came to us by way of Locke and the other defenders of the English revolution of 1688. It is the notion which goes back to Aristotle that the constitution brings to light and expresses the real character of

the body politic. Aristotle even goes so far as to maintain that the destruction of one constitution and the
substitution for it of a new constitution of a radically
different sort actually destroys the continuity of national life. What was one nation becomes another.[12]

If the constitution is the source of the national personality, then we have in Hooker the ancestor of Burke,
and we have in Burke the ancestor of the maturer view
of the American Constitution. That notion appears in
Webster when he debated Hayne, and in the post-
Civil War notion of the national existence. The United
States is not a mere confederation; it is a national personality, indissoluble and perpetual. It is a corporate
personality with a character all its own. Despite his
stress on the contractual origin of the state, Hooker
believes with Burke and the recent American consti-
tutionalists that the body politic is a legal personality.

Let us examine this concept of legal personality a
little more carefully. It is a rather complicated notion,
born of the insight of a man who knew the speculations
of the law schools. Like Aristotle, Hooker thought that
man was by nature social. The desire to associate with
other persons is native to man; and so society is not an
artifact. It springs from social inclinations, found in
every man and resulting quite naturally in the family
and in society.[13] Hooker does not subscribe to that
legal conception of Hobbes that social groups are the
result of the surrender of the individual's natural autonomy. Hooker does not recognize such independence,
because he believes that everything which exists tends
to work in co-operation with other things.[34] Man is no
exception to this general rule. The cohesion of society,
therefore, is not derived from the contract or constitution.

For Hooker that contract which is the constitution springs from the delegation of sovereignty by a society to a government. Here he is the very opposite of Hobbes. Hobbes thinks that sovereignty rests upon the individual and is then delegated to the ruler. Hooker thinks that sovereignty rests in society and is delegated to the ruler. The constitution, then, is the form in which that natural sovereignty which rests in society is delegated to those who rule it.[15] It is the constitution which gives personality or form to the group life. Otherwise, there would be a mob without any recognized form. It is the way of ruling which gives orientation to the group. It is the leaders who give direction to the life of the people.

This conception is very close to that of Aristotle, because Aristotle also recognizes that the state is to some extent a construct. Aristotle sounds like Hooker when he says, "Man is thus intended by nature to be a part of a political whole, and there is therefore an immanent impulse in all men towards an association of this order. But the man who first *constructed* such an association was none the less the greatest of benefactors."[16] The difference lies in the fact that Aristotle thinks that in a given organization some people naturally rule. Their ability manifests itself in such a way that they triumph over the less competent; and thus the form of rule is natural to a given kind of society. Of course a good rule may be perverted; but in a given kind of society its socio-economic life makes a certain kind of normal society inevitable. Hooker, on the other hand, thinks that government is much more a matter of choice; he thinks of the group by explicit reflection surrendering sovereignty to its rulers. That is, that natural sovereignty which belongs to the group is delegated to those who rule.

This same conception is found in a maturer form in American constitutional thinking. We too think of sovereignty as resting in the people: the conception that the individual is the locus of sovereignty has given way to the notion that sovereignty rests in society. We do not believe as did Aristotle that there is a natural sovereignty which belongs by nature to natural rulers. We too follow the tradition that sovereignty is delegated. Thus we are completely committed to the principle that sovereignty rests in the people and is delegated by them to the ruler. We are so committed to this notion that we desire an organic relationship between the people as the source of all sovereignty and their rulers.

Hooker himself is so completely committed to this notion of derived power that he separates the sovereignty exercised by the king from that exercised by parliament. Parliament receives its power directly from the people, and does not derive it from the throne. Here we have the origin of the constitutional principle of the separation of powers between the executive and the legislative branches of government. Hooker even thinks that the executive's power should be exercised primarily in the veto of legislative acts. Here we have the prototype of the American separation of the powers of government. It is a conception of the best manner of delegating the powers of the sovereign people.

Hooker transmitted to us the medieval notion of the sovereignty of the people delegated to those who rule, and so delegated that the will of the people is expressed by those who govern. It is the constitution which gives character to the nation by expressing the purpose of the national life through a certain kind of rule. For us, as for Hooker, the constitution is supreme.

Hooker and National Sovereignty

Much of Hooker's conception of the constitution goes back to Bracton, but there is one point in which Hooker does not follow the medieval lawyers. In this he is the follower of the Henrician reformation. The lawyers around Henry VIII found no English precedent for the dissolution of the ties which bound the kingdom to the Papacy; but they did find a precedent in Roman-Byzantine law. It is noteworthy that on the Continent there was a wide acceptance of the Roman law for the entire legal system. Those countries which remained loyal to the Roman Church adjusted Byzantine law to their purpose. The Lutheran countries also found in Roman-Byzantine law a system well adapted to their needs. It gave them precedents for a system which made national sovereignty final and allowed for many national churches in place of one international ecclesiastical jurisdiction. In the East the Orthodox church was divided into several national churches with fellowship between them, but without a central jurisdiction.

The lawyers around Henry VIII kept the older English law; they did not adopt the *Corpus Juris Civilis* and make it into an English system. Of course, there were those who would have desired such a legal reformation; and the English did study Roman law and set up a chair of Roman law at Oxford. There was a constant influence of the Civilians. It influenced the Anglo-Saxon conception of equity and gave precedent for the national state. Otherwise, the medieval law was intact.

In the matter of the sovereignty of the throne, the Henrician lawyers used Roman law: they increased the authority of the king and repudiated all international jurisdiction over the state. That means that they repudiated the authority of the Pope over the English king. It is easy to see how this centralization of government and the repudiation of the international power of the Pope made possible the development of what is called the sovereignty of the nation. This concept becomes one of the most significant of all future notions in Anglo-American law; and the jealous guardianship of sovereignty has been one of the most conspicuous features of English and American legal history.

As Lacey points out — and this is a notion developed by Figgis—not only was Roman law influential in this development of the sovereign national state, but the study of Aristotle's *Politics* gave a theoretic and idealistic phase to it.[17] The revolt of Henry was an empiric matter, but the development of national sovereignty also had in it a philosophical phase. The revival of Aristotle and Roman-Byzantine precedent gave to modern England and America an Aristotelian notion of the independent and self-sufficient state. As Lacey says:

The Schoolman discovered Aristotle, and in Aristotle the notion of a completely independent and self-sufficing city as the normal form of association for all the higher purposes of human life. The conception of the *societas perfecta* emerged, and was applied first to that unitary Christian commonwealth of which men dream, then by Bartolus of Sassoferrato to the civic republics of Italy, and finally to the

Church and state alike as men became conscious of their separate existence.[18]

Hooker becomes the classical exponent of the national state, but of the national state conceived in constitutional terms. He does not believe that the state possesses all power. The reason is that where a proper constitution prevails the people delegate power to those who rule and by the constitution limit that rule.[19] Hooker does not favor what Figgis calls the *omnicompetent state;* but what Hooker is stressing is essentially Aristotelian, and it is interesting that he quotes Aristotle to prove his point:

Many of the ancients in their writings do speak of kings with such high and ample terms, as if universality of power, even in regard of things and not of persons only, did appertain to the very being of a king. . . . But the most judicious philosopher, whose eye scarce any thing did escape which was to be found in the bosom of nature, he considering how far the power of one sovereign ruler may be different from another's regal authority, noteth in Spartan kings, "that of all others lawfully reigning they had the most restrained power." . . . Happier that people whose law is their king in the greatest of things than that whose king is himself their law. Where the king doth guide the state, and the law the king, the commonwealth is like an harp or melodious instrument, the strings whereof are tuned and handled all by one, following as laws the rules and canons of musical science.[20]

Here we have Hooker's Aristotelianism, for in the very same chapter in which he discusses the autonomous state, he also discusses the constitutional limitation of the royal power. Hooker's whole conception of the state is even more Aristotelian than is St. Thomas' notion. Hooker continues the interpretation of the state which St. Thomas began; but he uses even more of Aristotle than did the Angelic Doctor. The result is the conception of the autonomous sovereign state but that state under constitutional law. Hooker uses the medieval heritage, a heritage already interpreted in part by the Aristotelian method; and he makes his conception of the state even more Aristotelian. This is the Renaissance aspect of Hooker's thought.

This conception of the state, a conception which was more Aristotelian than that of St. Thomas, could appeal to Aristotle for support of the medieval doctrine that the best state is that in which the people consent to the rule over them. There is a strong constitutional strain in Aristotle, and he understands that no nation is happy if the rule over it is not accepted willingly.[21] The doctrine of the consent of the governed can be given an Aristotelian interpretation; and so it is by Hooker. It is through Aristotle that the conception of the autonomous national state is given a philosophic turn which saves it from that tyranny with which the Tudors and the Stuarts threatened it.

This is the conception of the state which has become the ancestor of our American theory of a constitutionally governed commonwealth. It is a medieval conception modified by many influences, but particularly by the organic conceptions of Aristotle. Our modern notion is not unlike that of Burke, and both Burke and we are heirs of Richard Hooker. The American Constitution as it is interpreted by the Supreme Court is more and more organic and more and more Aristotelian. We are the heirs, then, of both antiquity and the Middle Ages; and as heirs of both we are the descendants of Richard Hooker. Hooker is Janus-faced: he uses the medieval legal tradition, but he interprets it in terms of Aristotelian national sovereignty. In this we are his followers, and so for us Hooker is the true progenitor of the American Constitution.

1. Houk, Hooker's Ecclesiastical Polity Book VIII 7 (1931).
2. Pound, Interpretations of Legal History 103 (1923).
3. Whitehead, Science and the Modern World 13 ff. (1925).
4. Bayne, Of the Laws of Ecclesiastical Polity, the Fifth Book 596, n. 25 (1902).
5. XIII, 673.
6. Northrop, The Meeting of East and West 177 ff. (1946).
7. Hooker, Of the Laws of Ecclesiastical Polity V. ix. 3.
8. *Ibid.*, VIII. ii. 13.
9. Sisson, The Judicious Marriage of Mr. Hooker and the Birth of the Laws of Ecclesiastical Polity (1940).
10. Houk, *op. cit. supra,* n. 1, 86.
11. *Ibid.,* 85 ff.
12. Aristotle, Politics 1276b 1 ff.
13. Hooker, *op. cit. supra,* n. 7, I. x. 1.
14. *Ibid.,* I. iii. 5.
15. *Ibid.,* I. x. 8.
16. Aristotle, Politics 1253a 29 ff.
17. Lacey, Wayfarer's Essay 120 ff. (1934).
18. *Ibid.,* 121.
19. Hooker, *op. cit.* I. x. 4.
20. *Ibid.,* VIII. ii. 12.
21. Aristotle, Politics 1296a 13.

THE GHOST OF
HERBERT SPENCER: A DARWINIAN
CONCEPT OF LAW

Arthur L. Harding

AT this point in the discussion it would be more
in keeping with chronology to relate the story of how
the great medieval tradition of Natural Law was
transmuted in the seventeenth century to a doctrine
of Natural Rights. The change was subtle. The content of the new Natural Rights doctrine so closely
resembled that of the Natural Law as stated by medieval jurists that to the superficial observer there appeared to be no change. In methodology, however,
the new doctrine as formulated by Grotius broke
sharply from tradition. Eliminated was any idea that
Natural Rights rested upon the will of God, or that
a revealed divine plan might be studied for the discovery of content. To the contrary, Natural Rights were
derived from a cosmos of which God was but a part
and were the manifestations of a Natural Law to
which God Himself was subject.[1] Thus it was that one
hundred and fifty years after Grotius, the author of
the American Declaration of Independence appealed
not to Divine Providence, but to "the Laws of Nature
and of Nature's God."

Grotius followed in the tradition of his predecessors
in his reliance upon human reason to disclose the
nature and extent of Natural Rights. In the hands

of his followers, however, this appeal to reason became more and more subjective, with an increasing resort to intuition in the place of reason. So again the author of the American Declaration was to proclaim as "self-evident" the "certain unalienable Rights" there set forth.[2]

The story of the vicissitudes of the Natural Law in the seventeenth and eighteenth century era of Rationalism is a long and involved one, and must await a later day. Particularly to be examined is the suggestion, not infrequently made today, that the Rationalists, far from establishing a new era of human liberty, actually set the stage for a process of deterioration which, if unchecked, will destroy the very liberty which they asserted.[3]

Continuity of Terminology

It has become apparent in the foregoing discussions that while the terminology of Natural Law has been virtually unchanged through the centuries, the connotations and sometimes even the denotations of the words have been subject to change. So in Justinian's *Digest* we find that sometimes Natural Law means the magnificent Stoic concept of order as reflected by Cicero, and at other times means merely the *jus gentium,* the common jural experience of divers peoples in divers environments. In other hands Natural Law means simply the command of a living God.

Always present is the problem of how far the Natural Law, as the determinant of the Right and of the Just, is to be associated with the apparent laws of the physical nature which surrounds us. Even a trained thinker will display great confidence when dealing with phenomena that are evident to the five senses, but will become hesitant when dealing with facts that can be known only through reason, or which must be predicated upon faith. Still more significantly, the less well-trained mind may be hardly conscious of the problem. To this mind Natural Law is manifest in nature, and nature is the physical environment in which men live. Nature as the source or essence of life, the force that creates the phenomena of the physical world, is a concept little appreciated and even less understood.[4] The limitations of the language and the resulting problems of semantics are considerable. In any event, however, this mode of thinking cannot be dismissed lightly. As a social institution law, and therefore legal thinking, cannot but reflect popular terminology and popular beliefs. The identification in the popular mind of Natural Law with the laws of physical nature is a phenomenon which every jurist must take into account.

Influences of the Natural Sciences on Legal Thought

History tells us that developments in the fields of the natural sciences have had a profound effect upon the development of legal thought. The Rationalism of the seventeenth and eighteenth centuries was developed in close parallel to the development of the modern philosophy of science. The development of Newtonian physics and its companion, modern mathematics, led Comte to formulate a sociological theory of a society governed by natural laws as inflexible as those of mathematics. On the basis of Comte, jurists erected a positivist theory of law, fatalistic and unyielding, and appealed to Nature to support it. The great era of exploration and discovery which followed the voyages of Columbus led to the development of the science of ethnology. Following in the footsteps of the ethnologists were jurists who sought similarities and parallels in the social and juristic experiences and institutions of primitive and isolated peoples. On the basis of discoveries so made, these jurists gave the Roman concept of *jus gentium* a new content of legal thought common to all men irrespective of environment, and they called the result Natural Law.

Even in our own country, within the last century, we have seen a similar development. The discoveries of modern psychology, with its emphasis upon human desire and its theories of group will and group personality, led quite naturally to the American philosophy of pragmatism. Upon this philosophy of pragmatism was erected a sociological method of jurisprudence, in which the ends of law were principally two: to satisfy the desires of the individual human being, and to maintain an ordered control of the subgroups constituting the society.[5] Certainly today our admiration for the empirical methods of the natural sciences fathers a demand that the methods of jurisprudence likewise be placed upon an empirical foundation.

Of all the doctrines of the natural sciences which have influenced modern legal thought, perhaps the most significant is that of Darwin, and it is to Darwin that we turn.

Development of Darwinism

In studying a segment of human history, it is always difficult to know just where to start. We shall begin here in 1798 when a thirty-two-year-old Anglican cleric, Thomas Malthus, published his *Essay on Population*. His thesis was a pessimistic one: that human society is not perfectible; that realization of the dream of a happy society will always be hindered by the tendency of human population to increase at a rate far outdistancing the increase in the means of subsistence. Fascinated by the marvels of geometric progression, he found the greatest threat to the welfare of mankind to be its tendency to reproduce its own kind in ever increasing numbers. In his view mankind was doomed to a perpetual struggle for existence in the face of limited subsistence. Famine, disease, and war were not only the natural results of this struggle, but were necessary to assure minimum subsistence for those who survived. From this Malthus drew the rather startling conclusion that doles to the poor, particularly to the numerous children of the poor, were wrong. Far from curing any evil, these doles merely increased the number of mouths without increasing the amount of food, thereby aggravating the problem. In later writings Malthus added moral restraint as an additional limitation upon growth of population, meaning thereby a tendency in low subsistence areas toward celibacy, late marriages, and sexual abstinence, much as is the case in the Ireland of today.

For more than fifty years Malthus enjoyed a tremendous popularity, but then it began to be felt that the developments of modern technology had made his theories obsolete. Improved techniques bred an increasing confidence that mankind could sustain itself in ever greater numbers. However, one should keep in mind that in recent years there has been a marked revival of interest in Malthus and in his theories. Even

today there are those who warn of the dire consequences which are to flow from the introduction of
modern medical techniques into crowded Eastern
countries. There are those who feel that they are
performing a moral obligation and serving the social
good when they seek means to limit the production
of children by poor families.

In October, 1838, a copy of Malthus' *Essay on Population* fell into the hands of twenty-nine-year-old
Charles Darwin, and in it the reader found what he
considered to be the key to his own special problem.
From 1831 to 1836 young Darwin had served as na-
turalist on the ship *Beagle* on a protracted journey
of exploration to remote places in the southern hemis-
phere. Long before this voyage was concluded Darwin
came to believe that the neat doctrine of gradual
and orderly change, then a standard part of the scientific credo, failed utterly to explain the myriad forms
and variations in living things in the tropics. Two facts
were particularly troublesome. The first was that there
appeared to be few universal species; that each species
appeared somehow to be adapted to the place where
it was found. Second was the prodigious fertility of
nature in producing living things in the tropics, while
at the same time so few of these things lived to matur-
ity.

To explain these facts was the task which Darwin
set for himself in 1837. Darwin himself has said that
the explanation was found in Malthus, in the concept
of a struggle to survive in the face of inadequate means
of subsistence. In such a situation, Darwin concluded,
"favorable variations would tend to be preserved, and
unfavorable ones destroyed. The result of this would
be the formation of a new species."

By 1842 Darwin had formulated the theory that he sought: At best the earth can sustain only a small fraction of the organisms which the power of reproduction will bring forth. Inevitably many will perish. Also inevitably, those which survive will be those best adapted to the environment in which they struggle. Those varieties poorly adapted will perish at once, and in time those indifferently adapted likewise will be eliminated. And so is reached a natural law, an impersonal and inexorable law of natural selection, which determines the varieties which are to survive. Those that survive are the ones that reproduce and tend to transmit the characteristics which made survival possible. By 1857 Darwin had completed what he considered to be the scientific verification of his theory, and in 1859 his *Origin of Species* was published. Its publication set in motion new chains of thought in all fields of human endeavor, and unleashed intellectual forces which continue far from spent to this day.

The idea of evolution was not startling in 1859. That the physical world, living things in the world, and the social milieu of mankind were in process of change had become apparent. Under the label of "development" many theories and explanations had been put forth.[6] Astronomers had formulated theories of cosmic evolution. Geological theories of the development of the earth were well known. The Frenchman Buffon had explored the effect of environment upon animal species. Not long before Darwin, Lamarck had stated a theory of organic evolution based upon the assumed inheritance of acquired characteristics. Philosophers in most fields of inquiry approached the Hegelian concept of the inevitability of change or progress in line with an intellectually foreseeable pattern. On the practical side, the facts of the selective breeding of livestock were well known.

Thus the tremendous impact of Darwin's theory, setting off one of the great scientific debates of history, was not due to the idea of evolution. Rather it was due to three things: its apparent vindication of the scientific basis of Malthus' theory of population; its calm acceptance of the necessity of eliminating most living things that the remainder might flourish; and its stress upon chance as determining survival and directing change. It was in this last item that Darwin struck a gigantic blow at almost all philosophies and beliefs of his time. His predecessors had accepted the idea of change and development in both organic and inorganic nature, but they accepted it as an ordered or even predestined thing, flowing from the mind of God, or from the inexorable workings of some first cause or Logos which antedated or perhaps controlled God. The Hegelians accepted the idea of an evolution of the Good, but it was an evolution toward an ascertainable goal, driven by an idea of Good which was becoming more and more discernible in the course of history. To uproot these ideas of plan or order, and to substitute chance, was Darwin's truly revolutionary contribution.[7]

Herbert Spencer

The link between Darwin and the law was Darwin's English contemporary, Herbert Spencer, a self-taught philosophical radical, sometimes listed among the founders of modern sociology. Spencer accepted wholeheartedly the Utility principle of Jeremy Bentham, and was content to find a standard of values in the happiness of the individual human being. Spencer's ideal man, however, was primarily an economic man, and Spencer accepted the free-market economy of the laissez faire theory. It is not too far from correct to suggest that Spencer's acceptance of Utility and laissez faire was too enthusiastic, that he carried both ideas to an extreme which neither Bentham nor Adam Smith would have approved.

Like young Darwin, young Spencer also read Malthus' *Essay on Population* and was moved by its implications. Thenceforward, Spencer's thinking of human society was always in terms of a struggle for survival. Young Spencer likewise read and accepted the pre-Darwinian writings on biological development. He was fully conscious of the effect of environment on living organisms. He accepted from Lamarck the notion of purposive adaptation to environment, and of the transmission to progeny of the characteristics so acquired. However, the underlying theme of Spencer's evolution was teleological, an assumption of a dynamic plan or purpose. Here Spencer affected mysticism in a nodding obeisance to the Unknowable, seemingly not concerned to carry the inquiry further.

In 1850, nine years before Darwin's *Origin of Species*, Spencer published his *Social Statics*, setting forth his version of the ideal state. This ideal society was indeed static; it was one in which man had reached a perfect state of equilibrium with his environment. The first stage in the development of such a society is one in which man is in ceaseless struggle with both his environment and other men. In this stage violence is the principal obstacle to human happiness, and the state is necessary to control and limit violence. As the struggle continues, the less fit lose in the struggle and are eliminated, while the survivors become more and more adapted to their environment. As this development continues, there is less and less need for the state, and man can be left more and more free to pursue his own interests in the exercise of what have become his "natural rights." Projected logically, Spencer's theory leads to a withering away of the state in a manner remarkably similar to the manner in which Engels projected Marxist socialism. As of Spencer's own time, he considered the state to have only two internal functions: the control of an occasional outlaw, and the enforcement of economic undertakings.

Spencer's theory of the state is really little more than a catalogue of what the state should not do. The state is not to control economic activity. The state is not to engage in economic activity, such as the conduct of the post office or the operation of a public mint. Poor relief, safety legislation, social security legislation, all are condemned as interfering with the orderly processes of natural selection. Public education is bad as interfering with the process of selection, and of no affirmative value as a safeguard against evildoing. Public sanitation is condemned as tending to keep alive the weaker type, which might better perish for the benefit of mankind as a whole. Here then was a philosophy of "rugged individualism" with a vengeance. Strange and startling as it sounds today, it nevertheless was put forth by a respected and earnest man as the surest way to the achievement of human happiness.

The effect of Darwin and Spencer on each other was great. In Darwin, Spencer found what he considered to be scientific proof of what was merely a hypothesis in Malthus. Thereafter Spencer was to con-

sider the struggle for survival to be the prime motivation of human activity, and was to accept natural
selection as a measure of good. Thereafter Spencer
was to pay less and less attention to the concept of
purpose in social evolution, and to refer less and less
to the Unknowable as the motivation in evolution.
Increasingly he accepted Darwin's thesis of chance as
the determining factor.[8] On the other hand, Darwin
found in Spencer an ethical justification for his theory
of natural selection. The religious doubts which beset
Darwin in his early period became less and less notice-
able. Particularly to be noted was Darwin's acceptance
of Spencer's phrase "survival of the fittest" as epitomiz-
ing Darwin's theory. It was this phrase which was to
lead to a considerable misunderstanding of the implications of Darwin.

Reception of Spencerism in America

The widespread acceptance of Spencer's theories in
the United States was an outstanding phenomenon
of the latter part of the nineteenth century.[9] The
relation of this fact to the acceptance of Darwin is
important. The publication of the *Origin of Species* set
off what was perhaps the most notable scientific debate
in American history. American scientists were divided
sharply on the issue. Over a period of time, however,
Darwin's critics were overcome, and his theory was
accepted as true, subject of course to considerable
modification in detail. Those who accepted Darwin
as valid in the field of natural science were predisposed
to accept Spencer as stating truth in the social sciences.[10] Many, even of those who were critical of
Darwin, were ready to embrace Spencer as a proper

compromise between the new theory and the old. Those whose religious beliefs were offended by Darwin could find in the purposiveness of Spencer's *Social Statics* a confirmation of the existence of a divine plan in the evolution of the physical world. Spencer's vague references to the Unknowable were particularly pleasing to those whose faith was shaken by the seeming scientific truth of the observations of Darwin and his followers.

Spencer may not have been a great philosopher, but he had in great measure what so many philosophers lack: an ability to express his ideas in straightforward language easily understood by even the casual reader. Furthermore, it is to be noted that the extreme individualism of Spencer agreed closely with the Puritan and Calvinist theology generally accepted in America. His description of the struggle for survival in the economic arena closely followed the actuality of life on the American frontier. It appealed particularly as a philosophy fitted to the rapidly burgeoning industrialization of post-bellum America, giving to that industrialization a seeming ethical justification for some of its more ruthless and less pleasant aspects.

Whatever the causes, we do know that during Spencer's lifetime almost four hundred thousand volumes of his writings were sold in the United States. A lecture tour in the United States, sponsored by Andrew Carnegie, became the triumphant procession of a great hero. Later a posthumous eighteen-volume edition of Spencer's collected works enjoyed a wide sale. That a lusty, growing America had found its prophet appeared to be without question.

The defects of Spencer's reasoning and the invalidity of some of his observations have long since been exposed.[11] The ruthless fang-and-claw combination of economic individualism and natural selection formulated by Spencer and taught by others under the label of Social Darwinism is commonly said to have been discredited completely. Nevertheless, Social Darwinism has not been extirpated from the public mind. To the contrary, many of its ideas have been passed to successive generations as fundamental truths, resting upon both scientific and ethical necessity.[12] Popularly accepted as being in conformity with the processes of nature, these ideas came in time to be labeled natural laws, and ultimately tended to be established in the sacrosanct position accorded by the people of the country to those concepts of Natural Law derived from the older traditions.

Thomas McIntyre Cooley

In the first half of the nineteenth century the principal concern of the evolving American constitutionalism was the proper delimitation of the possibly overlapping functions of the state and federal governments. There was little occasion to come to the defense of those human liberties derived from the neoclassical doctrines of Hooker, Coke, and Locke, for those liberties were little challenged. In the second half of the century, however, such issues did come to the fore, and the proper delimitation of the powers of government with respect to individuals became the principal task. The authoritative thesis for this age was supplied in 1868 with the publication by Thomas M. Cooley of his *Treatise on the Constitutional Limitations Which Rest upon the Legislative Powers of the States of the American Union*. Under the familiar title of

Cooley on Constitutional Limitations, the book was to go through six editions in the author's lifetime and to be the most influential lawbook of the period.[13] Additionally, as a long-time judge of the Supreme Court of Michigan and as Dean of the University of Michigan Law School, considered by many the pre-eminent law school of the era, Cooley was to be the most influential jurist of his time.

Cooley's background is significant. He was one of a large family forced to labor hard on a poor farm to achieve subsistence. The struggle for existence of which Malthus and Spencer and Darwin wrote was real in Cooley's memory and experience. Largely self-educated, the young Cooley had probed deeply into classical and near-classical writings. His *Constitutional Limitations* abounds in references to Burlamaqui, to Locke, to Lieber, to Jefferson. The influence of Blackstone's Book I and of the writings of Lord Coke is evident. In formulating his doctrine of natural rights, Cooley departed little from the accepted statement. He adopted Locke's concept of organized society antedating government and conferring rights which are superior to government. His strong individualism was essentially that of Bentham, but was colored somewhat by the Spencerian concept of the inevitability of the struggle of individual man against other men. Cooley's concept of the role of the political state, of the legal order, was essentially the negative one of Spencer: to maintain a certain minimum of public order, to protect individuals seeking to further their individual interests in society, and to enforce economic bargains.

Cooley's significant contribution to the course of American law was to be found in the doctrine of *implied* limitations upon the powers of the state governments, and of an *implied* power in the courts to make these limitations effective. Notwithstanding that the state constitutions specified with considerable particularity the natural rights of individuals, Cooley asserted that there were other and implied limitations on legislative power which were to be found in the ethical concepts of previously existing organized society.[14] The implied limitations so read into the written constitution were to share with the written constitution the prestige of being the direct expression of the will of the people. The popular will so directly expressed was to be considered at all times paramount to the popular will as expressed indirectly through legislation. It was therefore the duty of the courts to strike down such legislation as would exceed the implied limitations upon the legislative power, even though no specific constitutional prohibition appeared to have been impinged.

Cooley accepted from Adam Smith the laissez faire assumption that the realization of private pecuniary motives will result in the public gain. The realization of monetary gain through economic activity was to be strictly a private affair from which government was to be barred, either as entrepreneur or as regulator. The struggle for economic advantage of individual over individual was strictly a private matter to which government could be only a bystander. Here Cooley's belief, sharply reflecting his own early life and experience, approached closely to that of Spencer.

Judge Cooley is sometimes labeled the prime supporter of Spencerian ethics in American law.[15] This may be unfair.[16] On the whole Cooley's work appears to be more accurately described as an assertion of the rationalist Natural Rights doctrine in a matrix of

Benthamite utilitarianism, but with a strong overtone of Spencerism becoming evident in discussions of economic interests. Cooley, however, is an important link in the course of development. His strong bias in favor of laissez faire economics undoubtedly facilitated the popular acceptance of Spencerism by seeming to give it the support of constitutional law. More importantly, his theory of implied limitations upon the power of government, and an implied power in the courts to make these limitations effective, set the stage for the next development which was undoubtedly Spencerian in its content.

Liberty of Contract

It has been seen that Spencerism or Social Darwinism came to America close on the heels of Darwinism. It came at a time when America was in an economic revolution. Sparked by the needs of the Civil War, industrialization was going forward at a rapid rate. The strains of readjustment were great. The accelerated growth of cities created new problems and brought forth demands for new legislation. The new industrialists, drinking for the first time the heady wine of economic power, were pushing forward relentlessly, sometimes ruthlessly, toward the realization and extension of that power. By the same token the newly developing laboring class, apprehensive of some courses of events, was turning to government for what was believed to be essential protection. Farmers, seeing their own power slip away, reacted similarly.

Quite naturally Spencerism was well received by the new industrialists, who could find therein an ethical justification for the necessity of ruthless competitive practices, resulting in the destruction of weaker competitors, or even in the near impoverishment of workers. Such things were thought of as contributing to the economic development of the nation. Andrew Carnegie was prominent in sponsoring Spencer and Spencerism in this country.[17] Others such as James J. Hill and the elder Rockefeller advanced Spencerism as justifying the moral necessity of publicly criticized business practices. Such, however, was the pervasiveness of the individualist faith and the gospel of the inevitability of human progress, that the acceptance of Spencerism was not confined to those who stood to gain by its adoption but extended to many whose interests would not be served thereby.

What economic interests were asserted in the name of Spencerism? They were several: a right to enter freely into any economic activity or vocation free of governmental restriction; a right to buy and sell goods *and services* on a free market without governmental interference; a right to borrow and lend money on a free market on whatever terms that market might establish; a right to combine or to associate with others to realize economic ends. These claims were not particularly new. Jeremy Bentham had advocated them as a key to human happiness under his Utility principle. In Bentham's system, however, these claims were not unlimited; rather they were subject to limitation in the protection of the happiness of others and for the public good. Spencer's contribution was to remove the limitations. According to the savage interpretation of Darwinism adopted by Spencer, the public good was not served by the protection of the economically weak against the economically strong. To the contrary, the economic welfare of the community would be enhanced

by removing from the field of economic activity those
less fitted to engage therein, just as the quality of the
race as a whole would be improved by eliminating
from the race its weaker members. Corollary propositions were that the power of taxation would not be
used to take gains from the economically successful
for the benefit of the economically unsuccessful; that
the powers of government would not be used to aid
one individual or class of individuals in economic
dealings with other individuals or classes; and that
government would not occupy any field of economic
activity so as to impair the ability of an individual to
enter that field.

Supporters of this Spencerian view found in Judge
Cooley's theory of constitutional limitations what they
thought to be legalistic support. The next task was
to establish Cooley's theory as the law of the land.
By coincidence, 1868, the year that saw the first publication of Cooley's work, saw also the adoption of the
Fourteenth Amendment to the United States Constitution with its injunction that no state should deprive any person of his life, liberty, or property without due process of law. Only four years after the
adoption of that Amendment a brilliant lawyer, John
A. Campbell, was to argue to the United States Supreme Court in the first of the Slaughterhouse cases[18]
that the Fourteenth Amendment embodied both the
Spencerian concept of a natural liberty of economic
activity and the Cooley doctrine of implied limitations upon leglislative power.[19] Attacking the validity
of a Louisiana statute establishing a slaughterhouse
monopoly in the New Orleans area, Campbell con-
tended that barring others from entering the slaughter-
ing business was a violation of the natural liberties of

the individual; and then that the Fourteenth Amendment clothed the United States Supreme Court with the power and duty to strike down the Louisiana statute. Campbell lost his battle but in the long run won the war. Two important Justices of the Court were converted to his view, Justice Bradley largely on the basis of arguments derived from Spencer and Cooley, and Justice Field largely on the basis of arguments derived from Adam Smith.[20] Thereafter in other cases these two were to advance Campbell's argument unceasingly until it prevailed as the doctrine of the majority of the court. The development, however, extended over a period of years.

Campbell's argument, which had failed in its initial appearance in the United States Supreme Court, was carried by others to the state courts and there met with considerable success. Thus, vindicating Campbell's contention, now bearing the label of Liberty or Right of Contract, state courts invalidated state legislation designed to fix the hours of labor, to require the payment of wages in cash in lieu of orders on a company store, to prohibit employers from interfering with membership in labor unions by their employees, to prohibit contracts by railway workers purporting to release the company in advance from any liability for injury to the workers, to prohibit the imposition of fines on employees, and other purposes.[21]

Finally in 1905, in a case involving the validity of a New York law limiting the workday of bakers to ten hours, Campbell's Spencerian-Cooley theory prevailed with a majority of the Justices of the Supreme Court and the statute was stricken down.[22] This was too much for Mr. Justice Holmes, whose own legal philosophy contained a substantial Darwinism.[23] In a caustic dissent Holmes referred bitingly to the "inarticulate major premises" of the majority opinion. He declared his belief that the case was "decided upon an economic theory which a large part of the country does not entertain" and asserted that "the Fourteenth Amendment does not enact Mr. Herbert Spencer's Social Statics."

The comparatively late date of the inclusion of Liberty of Contract among the natural rights of men is interesting. By 1905 Spencer was generally discredited as a philosopher. Among sociologists Spencer's tooth-and-claw sociology had been supplanted by Lester Ward's sociology of co-operation and intelligent control.[24] Certainly by 1905 Spencer had lost a considerable part of his popular following, and the idea of legislative regulation had gained support. Nevertheless the Court set forth to graft onto the older tradition of Natural Law an increasingly unacceptable concept of a natural right of contract supposedly derived from the laws of organic existence.

The remainder of the story is familiar history, told elsewhere in detail many times. Applying the theory the court in 1915 invalidated a state statute outlawing the "yellow-dog" contract,[25] and in 1923 rejected wage-fixing by statutory authority.[26] Also in 1923 was stricken down a minimum wage statute applicable to the District of Columbia,[27] and again in 1936 a state minimum wage statute fell.[28] The gulf between Court and the people appeared to be ever widening, with ever increasing criticism of the Court by those advocating legislative protection against claimed economic abuses. The final result of course was the court-packing controversy of 1937 and a possible reorientation of American legal theory.

In any event the Supreme Court in 1937 sustained the validity of a Washington statute fixing a minimum wage for women workers of $14.50 for a forty-eight-hour week.[29] The opinion by Chief Justice Hughes reaffirmed the Court's support of certain cases decided prior to the 1905 adoption of the Liberty of Contract theory, and repeated the 1898 statement that

the fact that both parties are of full age, and competent to contract, does not necessarily deprive the state of the power to interfere, where the parties do not stand upon an equality, or where the public health demands that one party to the contract shall be protected against himself. . . . The state still retains an interest in his welfare, however reckless he may be. The whole is no greater than the sum of all the parts, and when the individual health, safety and welfare are sacrificed or neglected, the state must suffer.[30]

The Court concluded by overruling the 1923 decision which had nullified a minimum wage statute for the District of Columbia.[31]

That the 1937 case was decided upon a reappraisal of the Spencerian doctrine may be seen by examining the dissenting opinion of Justice Sutherland, with its reliance upon Cooley's *Constitutional Limitations* and its reiteration of language from a 1908 opinion that

the right of a person to sell his labor upon such terms as he deems proper is, in its essence, the same as the right of the purchaser of labor to prescribe the conditions on which he will accept such labor from the person offering to sell. . . . In all such particulars the employer and employee have equality of right, and any legislation that disturbs that equality is an arbitrary interference with the liberty of contract which no government can legally justify in a free land.[32]

Epilogue

Whether the Spencerian theory of Liberty of Contract, or any substantial part of it, remains the law of the land is not known. Certainly Cooley's doctrine of implied limitations on governmental power continues to grow. In recent years the Fourteenth Amendment has been construed to encompass liberties of speech and press and religion to an extent which even Cooley would have thought impossible. That this has been accompanied by silence concerning any liberty of contract is perhaps most significant.

Whether or to what extent the concept of Liberty of Contract is a socially desirable one is not here determined. It seems reasonable to assume that economic progress is essential to civilization in the sense of enhancing the power of man over external nature. Certainly the reduction of social restraint upon individual economic activity is one means of achieving a measure of economic progress. What is criticized here is the transmutation of Liberty of Contract into the "unalienable," thereby preventing or limiting any pragmatic or reasoned inquiry into its social desirability in a particular setting. What is criticized also is the grafting upon a legitimate notion of a liberty of economic activity, of Darwin's ruthless process of natural selection. Even if Darwinism is to be applied, it has not been applied too intelligently. It must be remembered that the unhappy phrase "survival of the fittest" was Spencer's and not Darwin's, and that a good deal of the savagery of Social Darwinism was derived from the English Thomas Huxley and the American William Graham Sumner.[33] Later thinking upon cooperation as a means of adaptation, survival, and evolution of the species appears to have been considered not at all.

The moral of this story is simple. The classical and medieval tradition of Natural Law has given meaning to what is called Western civilization. The American people cling to a faith that there is such a Law. In this they are not alone. The cry for justice going up in many parts of the world necessarily reflects a belief that there is some standard and there is some agency by which justice may be measured and may be made effective. Any system of law or the ordering of society must take this belief into account. At the same time, however, it is an area in which one must move carefully and must avoid traps.

The Nature of Aristotle, of Cicero, of St. Thomas, and of Hooker was a good Nature, a goal of perfection to be sought by men on earth, and the Natural Law was a sort of guide toward that perfection. The nature of Spencer (spelled now with a small *n*) was ethically indifferent. It was, and was in the process of becoming. What it was in the process of becoming appears to have been unimportant. If we are to consider Nature as a source of law or as a part of law, we must consider it in all its aspects. It would be error to be willing to consider only the outward manifestations of physical nature around us; to be content to examine and to conform to those physical manifestations, while ignoring the causes and forces which produce those effects. The Social Darwinian told us that this was enough, and told us so in the language of the Natural Law that we might accept his conclusion unquestioningly. The Natural Lawyer bids us look further to first causes, to that which creates the laws of physical nature. We can hope only that the decision and choice may be intelligently made.

1. D'Entreves, Natural Law, Chapter III (1951).
2. Jefferson's rough draft read "sacred and undeniable" and "rights inherent & inalienable." As to the authorship of the changes, Boyd, The Declaration of Independence 22 (1945). Bainton, "The Appeal to Reason and the American Constitution," in The Constitution Reconsidered 121 ff. (Ed. Read 1938).
3. Brunner, Justice and the Social Order, Chapter I (Tr. by Hottinger 1945).
4. Jeans, The Mysterious Universe, Chapter V (1934).
5. Pound, "The Scope and Purpose of Sociological Jurisprudence," 25 Harv. L. Rev. 489 (1912).
6. Simpson, The Meaning of Evolution, Chapter XVI (1949).
7. Dewey, The Influence of Darwin on Philosophy, Lecture I (1910); Sears, Charles Darwin 73 ff. (1950); Blau, Men and Movements in American Philosophy, Chapter V "The Biologizing of Philosophy" (1952).
8. Hofstadter, Social Darwinism, Chapter II (1944). The individualism of Spencer should be contrasted with that of John Stuart Mill. Sabine, A History of Political Theory 721 ff. (Rev. ed. (1950).
9. If there be blame it must be shared by the American William Graham Sumner. Hofstadter, op. cit. supra n. 8, Chapter III.
10. Faris, "Evolution and American Sociology" in Evolutionary Thought in America 160 ff. (Ed. Persons 1950). Spencer's sociology is not the only application of Darwinism to human affairs. Huxley, Evolution in Action, Chapter VI (1953); Simpson, op. cit. supra n. 6, Chapter XVIII.
11. Patterson, "Historical and Evolutionary Theories of Law," 51 Col. L. Rev. 681, 700 (1951).
12. See, for example, the credo of middle-class Middletown, U.S.A., as reported by Lynd and Lynd, Middletown in Transition 408-410 (1937).
13. Twiss, Lawyers and the Constitution, Chapter II (1942).
14. Cooley, Constitutional Limitations 358 (8th ed. 1927): "The maxims of Magna Charta and the common law are the interpreters of constitutional grants of power, and those acts which by those maxims the several departments of government are forbidden to do cannot be considered within any grant or apportionment of power which the people in general terms have made to those departments." This and similar language by Judge

Cooley, closely approaching Sir Edward Coke's identification of Common Law with Natural Law, served to undermine what otherwise were quite proper statements of the role and function of courts in dealing with legislation of questioned constitutionality.

15. E.g., Twiss, *loc. cit. supra*, n. 9.

16. One should note, however, Paschal's study of the influence of Cooley on latter-day constitutional law through Justice Sutherland. Paschal, Mr. Justice Sutherland: A Man against the State (1951).

17. McCloskey, American Conservatism in the Age of Enterprise, Chapter VI (1951).

18. *Slaughterhouse Cases,* 111 U.S. 746 (1873).

19. Hamilton, "The Path of Due Process of Law," in The Constitution Reconsidered (Ed. Read 1938); Twiss, *op. cit. supra,* n. 13, 42 ff.

20. McCloskey, *op. cit. supra,* n. 17, Chapters IV and V.

21. A careful study of these cases is found in Pound, "Liberty of Contract," 18 Yale L. Jour. 454 (1909).

22. *Lochner v. New York,* 198 U.S. 45 (1905).

23. For the impact of Darwinism on Mr. Justice Holmes see Wiener, Evolution and the Founders of Pragmatism, Chapter VIII (1949).

24. Schneider, A History of American Philosophy, Chapter XXXIII (1946); Ashley Montagu, Darwin: Competition & Cooperation, Chapter I (1952).

25. That is, an agreement by a prospective employee not to join a labor union during the period of employment. *Coppage v. State of Kansas,* 236 U.S. 1 (1915).

26. *Charles Wolff Packing Co. v. Court of Industrial Relations of Kansas,* 262 U.S. 522 (1923).

27. *Adkins v. Children's Hospital,* 261 U.S. 525 (1923).

28. *Morehead v. New York,* 298 U.S. 587 (1936).

29. *West Coast Hotel Co. v. Parrish,* 300 U.S. 379 (1937).

30. Mr. Justice Brown in *Holden v. Hardy,* 169 U.S. 366 (1898), upholding a Utah statute which limited the underground work day of miners and the total workday of smelter workers to eight hours.

31. *Adkins v. Children's Hospital, supra* n. 27.

32. Mr. Justice Harlan in *Adair v. United States,* 208 U.S. 161 (1908), holding invalid an act of Congress designed to prevent discharge of employees of interstate carriers because of membership in labor unions.

33. *Supra,* n. 9.

INDEX